Shifra Stein's

DAY TRIPS®
FROM
GREATER BALTIMORE

Getaways
Less Than Two Hours Away

WRITTEN BY GWYN WILLIS
EDITED BY SHIFRA STEIN

The East Woods Press
Charlotte, North Carolina • Boston • New York

©1985 by Shifra Stein
First Edition

Second Printing, 1986

All rights reserved. No part of this book may be reproduced without permission from the publisher, except by a reviewer who may quote brief passages in a review; nor may any part of the book be reproduced, stored in a retrieval system or transmitted in any form or by any means, electronic, mechanical, photocopying, recording or other, without permission from the publisher.

Library of Congress Cataloging in Publication Data

Willis, Gwyn.
    Day trips from greater Baltimore.
    (Shifra Stein's Day trips)

    Includes index.
    1. Baltimore Region (Md.)—Description and travel—
Tours. 2. Middle Atlantic States—Description and travel—
tours. 3. Maryland—Description and travel—1981- —
Tours. I. Stein, Shifra. II. Title. III. Series: Stein,
Shifra. Day Trips America.
F189.B13W55   1985   917.52'0443   84-28778
ISBN 0-88742-023-0

Photographs by Robert Willis
Local maps by Sara Park Stuart
Cover design by Kenn Compton
Typography by Raven Type
Printed in the United States of America

The East Woods Press
Fast & McMillan Publishers, Inc.
429 East Boulevard
Charlotte, N.C. 28203

CONTENTS

Preface, 9

N O R T H

Day Trip 1
BALTIMORE
COUNTY, MD.: 14
Cloisters Children's Museum, 14
Rosa Ponselle Museum, 14
Sagamore Farm, 15
Hampton House, 15

Day Trip 2
BALTIMORE
COUNTY, MD.: 16
Loch Raven Reservoir, 16
Ladew Topiary Gardens, 16
Boordy Vineyards, 16

Day Trip 3
HERSHEY, PA., 18

Day Trip 4
KUTZTOWN, PA., 20
LANCASTER, PA., 20
(Pennsylvania Dutch Country)

Day Trip 5
READING, PA., 23
(Outlet Capital of America)

N O R T H E A S T

Day Trip 1
EDGEWOOD, MD., 28
ABERDEEN, MD., 29
HAVRE DE GRACE, MD., 29
PERRYVILLE, MD., 30
NORTHEAST, MD., 31
ELKTON, MD., 32

Day Trip 2
WILMINGTON, DE., 33
NEW CASTLE, DE., 35

Day Trip 3
PHILADELPHIA, PA., 37

Day Trip 4
THE BRANDYWINE VALLEY, PA., 39
WORTH MORE TIME:
VALLEY FORGE, PA., 41

CONTENTS

SOUTHEAST

Day Trip 1
ANNAPOLIS, MD., 46

Day Trip 2
CHESTERTOWN, MD., 51
CENTREVILLE, MD., 52
WYE MILLS, MD., 52

Day Trip 3
EASTON, MD., 54
OXFORD, MD., 55
ST. MICHAELS, MD., 57
WORTH MORE TIME:
BLACKWATER
NATIONAL
WILDLIFE
REFUGE, MD., 58

SOUTH

Day Trip 1
PORT TOBACCO, MD., 64
CHARLOTTE HALL, MD., 65
SMALLWOOD STATE PARK, MD., 65

Day Trip 2
ACCOKEEK, MD., 67
CLINTON, MD., 68
FORT WASHINGTON NATIONAL PARK, MD., 68

SOUTHWEST
And Washington Region

Day Trip 1
KENSINGTON, MD., 74
WHEATON, MD., 75
COLUMBIA, MD., 75

Day Trip 2
PRINCE GEORGE'S COUNTY, MD.:
Early Mansions Tour, 77

Day Trip 3
PRINCE GEORGE'S COUNTY, MD.:
Aerospace Tour, 80

Day Trip 4
WASHINGTON, D.C., 84
GEORGETOWN, D.C., 86

Day Trip 5
ARLINGTON, VA., 88
ALEXANDRIA, VA., 89
MT. VERNON, VA., 92
WORTH MORE TIME:
MANASSAS, VA., 94

CONTENTS

Day Trip 6
GREAT FALLS OF
THE POTOMAC, MD., 96
C&O CANAL NATIONAL
HISTORICAL PARK,
MD., 97

Day Trip 7
MIDDLEBURG, VA., 100
LEESBURG, VA., 101
WATERFORD, VA., 102
POINT OF ROCKS,
MD., 103

W E S T

Day Trip 1
ELLICOTT CITY, MD., 108
MOUNT AIRY, MD., 109
NEW MARKET, MD., 110

Day Trip 2
FREDERICK, MD., 111
LILY PONS, MD., 112
SUGAR LOAF
MOUNTAIN, MD., 113

Day Trip 3
HAGERSTOWN, MD., 114
BOONSBORO, MD., 115
SHARPSBURG, MD., 116
MIDDLETOWN, MD. 117

Day Trip 4
SHEPHERDSTOWN,
WV., 119
HARPER'S FERRY,WV., 121
WORTH MORE TIME:
CHARLES TOWN,WV., 124

N O R T H W E S T

Day Trip 1
REISTERSTOWN, MD., 128
WESTMINSTER, MD., 129
UNIONTOWN, MD., 131
NEW WINDSOR, MD., 132

Day Trip 2
EMMITSBURG, MD., 134
THURMONT, MD.: 135
Catoctin Mountain National Park, 136
Cunningham Falls State Park, 137

Day Trip 3
UNION MILLS, MD., 140
GETTYSBURG, PA., 141

FESTIVALS AND CELEBRATIONS, 144
THE GREAT OUTDOORS, 152
SEASONAL INFORMATION, 154
REGIONAL INFORMATION, 155

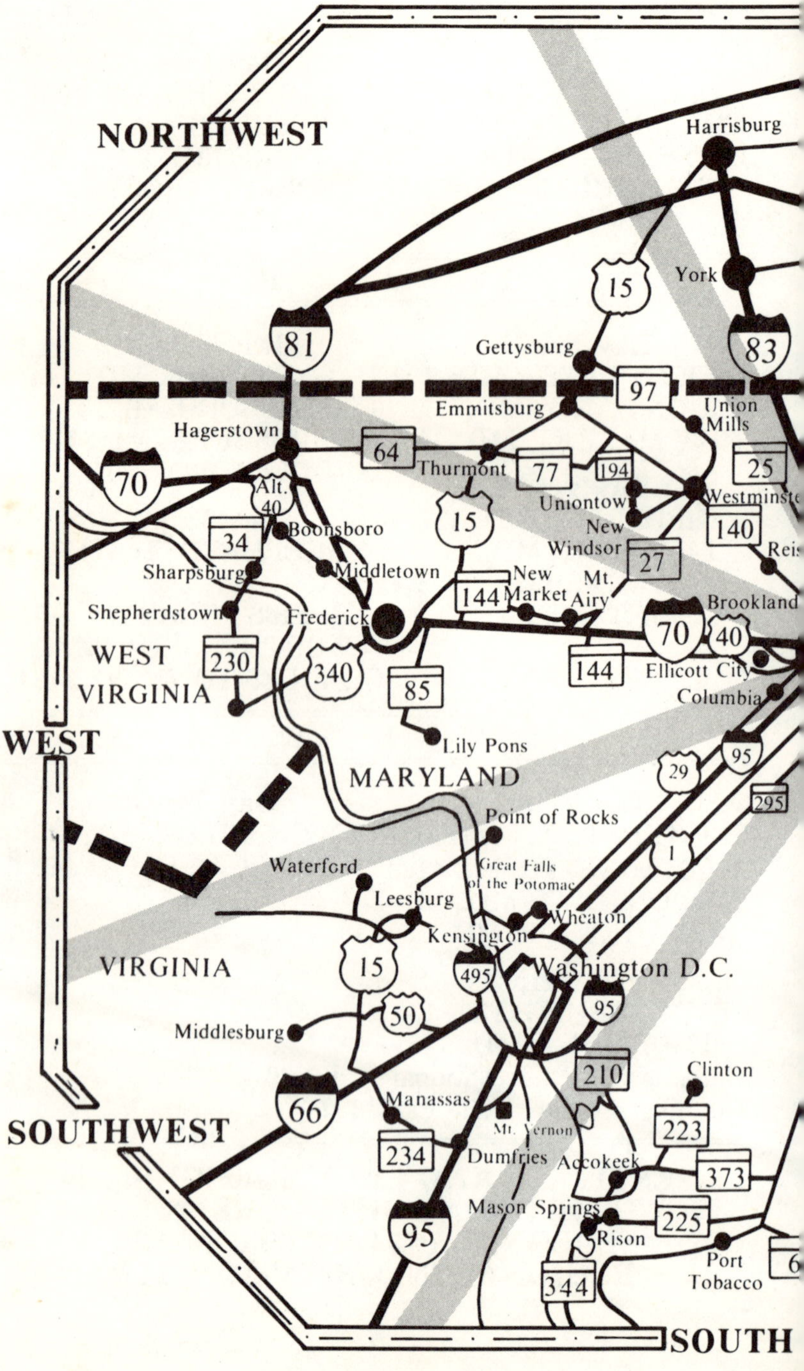

NORTHWEST
Harrisburg
York
15
81
83
Gettysburg
97
Emmitsburg
Union Mills
Hagerstown
64
70
Thurmont
77
194
25
Alt. 40
Uniontown
Westminster
34
Boonsboro
New Windsor
140
15
27
Sharpsburg
Middletown
New Market
Mt. Airy
144
Shepherdstown
Frederick
70
Brookland
40
WEST VIRGINIA
230
340
85
144
Ellicott City
Columbia
WEST
Lily Pons
95
29
MARYLAND
295
Point of Rocks
1
Waterford
Great Falls of the Potomac
Leesburg
Wheaton
Kensington
VIRGINIA
15
495
Washington D.C.
95
50
Middlesburg
210
Clinton
66
Manassas
Mt. Vernon
223
SOUTHWEST
234
Dumfries
Accokeek
373
Mason Springs
225
95
Rison
Port Tobacco
344
SOUTH

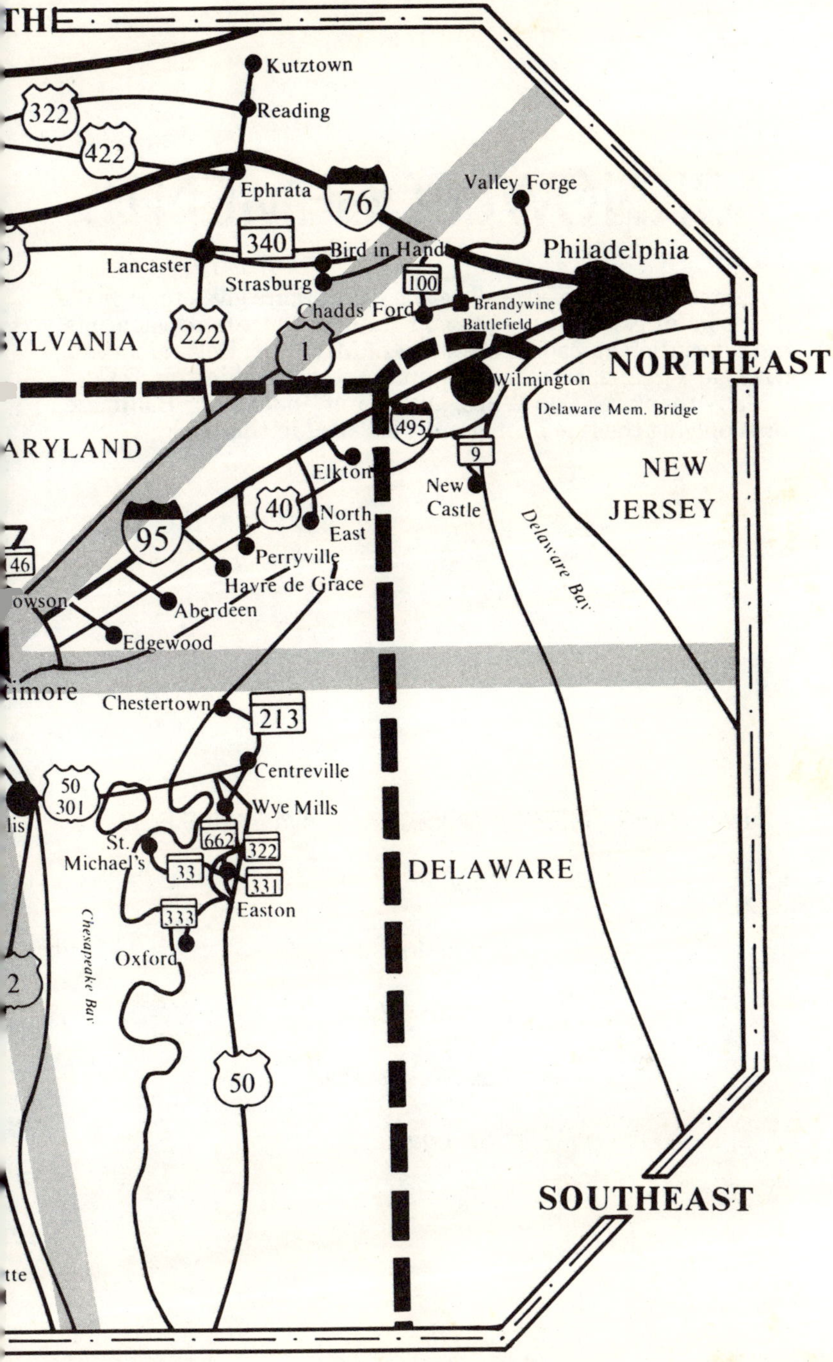
THE
Kutztown
Reading
322
422
Ephrata
76
Valley Forge
340
Lancaster
Bird in Hand
Strasburg
Philadelphia
100
Chadds Ford
Brandywine
Battlefield
SYLVANIA
222
1
NORTHEAST
Wilmington
Delaware Mem. Bridge
495
ARYLAND
Elkton
9
New
Castle
NEW
JERSEY
40
North
East
95
Delaware Bay
46
Perryville
Havre de Grace
owson
Aberdeen
Edgewood
timore
Chestertown
213
Centreville
50
301
Wye Mills
lis
St.
Michael's
662
322
33
331
DELAWARE
333
Easton
Chesapeake Bay
Oxford
2
50
SOUTHEAST
tte

ACKNOWLEDGEMENTS

We gratefully acknowledge all help and assistance given to us by the chambers of commerce, state and regional tourism departments, and convention bureaus of the states of Maryland, Delaware, Pennsylvania, Virginia, and West Virginia, and of Washington, D.C.

Many thanks to Bob Willis, Director of Tourism for Baltimore, for supplying the fine photographs included in this book.

DAY TRIPS AMERICA BOOKS ARE AVAILABLE FOR

Cincinnati

Houston

Kansas City

Minneapolis–St. Paul

St. Louis

PREFACE

Welcome to Maryland, a beautiful area that has played a great role in America's history. Here cemeteries have headstones that tell the stories of Revolutionary War patriots, and chronicles of Maryland's past tell of visits by Spanish Jesuit missionaries as far back as 1570!

With this Day Trips guide in hand, you'll travel through three centuries of history in southern Maryland. Special places here pay tribute to the agricultural heritage that still predominates in the region. This guide will lead you to rich landscapes, past Maryland's horse country, and through the open fields and pristine farmland that are part of the Pennsylvania Dutch area.

Along the way you can sample a variety of foods and Americana sold in wonderful shops and market places that dot Maryland and the nearby states of Pennsylvania, Virginia, West Virginia, and Delaware—all colorfully outlined in this book.

From agriculture and architecture to history and high tech—it's all here... and it's all near.

How to Use This Book
When using this guidebook, be sure to keep the following things in mind:

DRIVING TIME: Individual trips are designed as one-day, round-trip excursions with the farthest points within a two-hour drive from greater Baltimore. Sometimes the itinerary goes beyond that limit, as in the case of Charles Town, when we feel it is well "Worth More Time," as these destinations are titled.

MAPS: While maps are included in this guide, we highly recommend taking along state maps for more detailed information.

HIGHWAY DESIGNATIONS: Federal highways are designated "US." State routes are defined as follows: "M" for Maryland, "D" for Delaware, "P" for Pennsylvania, "WV" for West Virginia, and "V" for Virginia. Interstate routes are designated as "I".

RESTAURANTS: The symbol "$" means less than $8 per person; "$$" means $8 to $15 per person; "$$$" means more that $15 per person, not

PREFACE

including beverage, tax, or tip. The symbol "□" indicates that credit cards are accepted. "No □" indicates that major credit cards are not accepted.

HOURS: Because this guide must be prepared months in advance of printing, details such as hours and days of operation, which change frequently, could be obsolete by the time you read them. Therefore, we do not include days and hours of operation; we do include telephone numbers so you can call for up-to-date information.

COMBINING TRIPS: These trips are arranged so they may easily be combined into an excursion of more than one day. In several cases you could take one trip out and another trip back, or you could combine two or more day trips in the same sector.

FESTIVALS AND CELEBRATIONS: Check the directory in the back of the book to find out what's going on in the area before you head out. Telephone numbers are included so you can call for specific information.

As always, your suggestions for future editions are welcomed.

Shifra Stein
Editorial Director

To an apple that fell close to the tree

NORTH

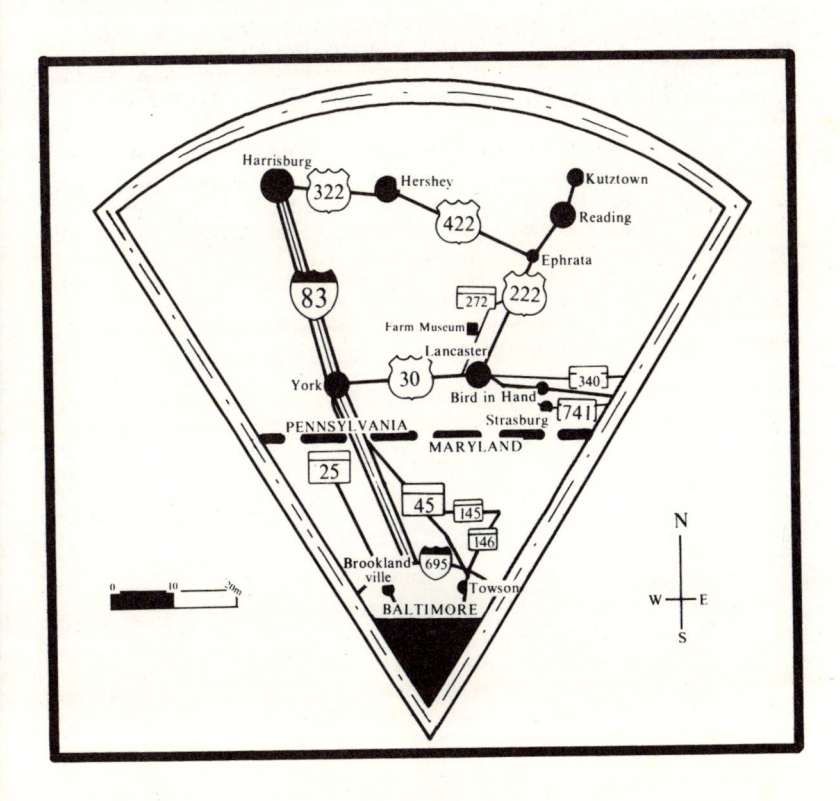

NORTH

North of Baltimore is the rich landscape of Maryland horse country and the birthplace of the champions at Sagamore Farms. Mother nature is at work in the Boordy Vineyards and the graceful, green extravaganza of Ladew Topiary Gardens. As suburbs yield to rolling countryside, sprawling farms, meadows, and woodlands, you'll see some of the most picturesque countryside in the state.

Pennsylvania's south central area has the state's capital, Harrisburg, as well as the open fields and pristine farmland of Amish country. Here, horse and buggies still travel the highways, recalling earlier times. This region's appeal isn't all history, though. Some of America's most enjoyable theme parks are located here. Fun for all ages awaits visitors seeking thrills and activities at Dutch Wonderland and Hershey Park. And (grab your pocketbook!) you'll be visiting the "factory outlet capital of the world." The York-Lancaster-Reading shopping triangle boasts a bounty of bargains.

Groaning boards laden with Pennsylvania Dutch cooking are a feast for the eyes and the appetite. Have your day trip dinner at one of the many smorgasbord-style restaurants featuring local, traditional fare. Take home tasty breads and pies from the colorful Amish markets as you wind your way home from your trip to the north.

Hampton House National Historic Site

N O R T H

Day Trip 1

BALTIMORE COUNTY, MD.

Immediately north of the city of Baltimore lies the scenic countryside of Baltimore County. For day-trip drivers who want to stay relatively close to the city, this drive is pleasant, but not demanding—a perfect Sunday diversion. The range of attractions should include something for everyone in the family.

Take Falls Road north (M-25) out of Baltimore to get there.

WHERE TO GO

The Cloisters Children's Museum. 10440 Falls Road, Brooklandville, Md. On Falls Road north, cross the I-695 overpass and continue a short distance. Keep alert to avoid missing the quiet entrance in the trees on the left. The large French Gothic Tudor Revival castle was built in 1930 by Sumner Parker. Children of all ages will enjoy a visit to this country estate filled with medieval trappings and collections of antique clothing, masks, dolls, and doll houses. Special creative activities are frequently held here. A phone call may help you to choose just the right day to visit. Free. (301) 823-2551 or 823-2550.

The Rosa Ponselle Museum at "Villa Pace." Greenspring Valley Road, Stevenson. From Falls Road turn left onto Greenspring Valley Road and continue for exactly 2 miles to the Rosa Ponselle Museum sign on your right (across from Villa Julie College). "Villa Pace" was the home of diva Rosa Ponselle from 1941 until her death in 1981. The museum was established as a Center for the Arts in 1982. Visitors can see how the great American soprano lived and enjoy programs such as concerts, recitals, opera workshops, and lectures. This fascinating, cross-shaped Mediterranean villa is a reflection of a great woman: her life, her travels, and her art. Relish the expansive view from the bedroom balcony. The music room is exquisitely appointed in Scalamandre draperies. Its vaulted ceiling is made of hand-painted walnut panels. The foyer is dominated by a staircase

NORTH

accented with deep blue Cuban tiles leading to a balcony that overlooks the foyer. It was from this vantage that Miss Ponselle enjoyed spontaneous singing, and she claimed the foyer's acoustics were "marvelous." For all inquiries and tour information, call (301) 486-4616.

Sagamore Farm. Belmont Road, Glyndon. Take Greenspring Valley Road to Greenspring Avenue northwest. Turn right onto Tufton Avenue and then left onto Belmont Road. Welcome to horse country and the famous Vanderbilt Farm, established for the breeding and training of champion thoroughbreds. These stables have produced such greats as Native Dancer, Kauai King, Restless Dancer, and Globemaster. Green velvet pastures are laced with a network of spotless white fences. Slow your car to capture a memory of these beautiful grazing mares and their foals. The Maryland Hunt Cup, a point-to-point steeplechase, is held nearby each April. While the stables are private and not open for tours, much of the beauty can be appreciated as you drive by. Return via Tufton Avenue east to Falls Road south (M-25) to I-695 toward Towson.

Hampton House National Historic Site. 535 Hampton Lane, off Dulaney Valley Road, Towson. (I-695 exit at Dulaney Valley Road.) This is a magnificent late-Georgian mansion containing many of its original Federal and Empire furnishings. Stroll through the surrounding formal gardens with functional out-buildings. Free tour information. (301) 823-7054. For luncheon in the tearoom or on the patio, make reservations. (301) 823-9849.

Return to Dulaney Valley Road, turn left (south) to York Road and Baltimore.

WHERE TO EAT

Harvey's Restaurant. 2360 W. Joppa Road, Brooklandville. This property is well situated among the fascinating shops of the Greenspring Station, located near Falls Road and Greenspring Avenue. Careful attention to cheerful surroundings, color co-ordinated table settings, and competent serving staff add up to a pleasant dining experience. $-$$; ☐. (301) 296-9526.

The Valley Inn. 10501 Falls Road, Brooklandville. Just past the Cloisters Children's Museum on the right side of Falls Road is the stone, more-than-100-year-old structure of the quaint Valley Inn. Murals of Maryland life and the sport of dog racing grace the walls of friendly rooms. Fireplaces and hardwood floors blend with traditional Maryland cuisine. $$; ☐. (301) 828-8080.

N O R T H

Day Trip 2

BALTIMORE COUNTY, MD.

The northern corridor extends another invitation to sample scenes and sights of Baltimore County. Depart the city north on York Road (M-45) to Dulaney Valley Road (M-146) in Towson. We'll visit the natural beauty of a reservoir, the cultivated elegance of a topiary garden, and a vineyard and winery.

WHERE TO GO

Loch Raven Reservoir. Proceed north on M-146 from Towson for about 3.7 miles. Winding roads lead you through beautifully forested areas pervaded with the scent of pine. Breaks in the dense trees allow views of the 10-mile-long lake. The reservoir area, built in 1912, offers excellent picnic areas (no open fires), boating, fishing, and hiking activities. Sunday visits are especially nice for bikers and joggers, because on part of the thoroughfare regular traffic is blocked. Terrain is varied, so physical exercise potential is good. Free. Call the Baltimore County Department of Recreation and Parks, Lock Raven Community Office, (301) 828-1140.

Ladew Topiary Gardens. 3535 Jarrettsville Pike (M-146), Monkton. After passing Jacksonville, watch for the topiary gardens. Twenty-two acres of artfully planned gardens await you. Cited by the Garden Club of America as America's "most outstanding topiary garden," it features 15 seasonal blooming gardens. The world-famous topiary hedges feature a life-size topiary fox hunt with horse and rider. The hedges are clipped and patiently trained into the shapes of animals and other whimsical objects. The Manor House of the late Harvey Ladew, creator of the gardens, contains antiques, paintings, and objets d'art. The house and gardens are on the National Register of Historic Places. A gift shop and craft shop are on the premises. Fee. (301) 557-9466.

The Boordy Vineyards. 12820 Long Green Pike, Hydes. Take

Jarrettsville Pike (M-146) to Manor Road south and turn left. Continue on Manor to Long Green Pike east, and turn left to Hydes. Nestled in the hills of Baltimore County is the oldest vineyard in the country. The rustic barn surrounded by vineyards, stone patios, and pastures is a welcome departure from the fast urban pace. Here, grapes are picked, cleaned, crushed, and then aged in vintage oak casks.

Boordy produces a full line of dry table wines which excel at complementing food. They also offer a popular sweet variety of wine. The individual attention given to these wines includes hand-labeling each bottle. Production averages 5,000 cases a year. Knowledgeable guides direct visitors through the vineyards and winery. September visits are especially good, for this is the best time to see the harvesting and crushing. A picnic area is available. Notify Boordy in advance for group tours. No fee, but there is a tour charge for groups greater than 10. (301) 592-5015.

WHERE TO EAT

Peerce's Plantation. Dulaney Valley Road, 7 miles north of Towson. This scenic dining spot, located at the entrance to the watershed area of Loch Raven Reservoir, offers consistently fine food. The dining rooms have a view of the lake. $$-$$$; □. (301) 252-3100.

Ladew Topiary Gardens

N O R T H

Day Trip 3

HERSHEY, PA.

Chocolate lovers, beware—this town will satiate your senses! The sweet aroma pervades the town, designated the "chocolate capital of the world." The two main streets are—what else?—Chocolate and Cocoa Avenues, where streetlamps mimic chocolate kisses.

From Baltimore take I-83 to Harrisburg. Take US-322 east to Hershey. Then pick up P-743 north to the attractions in this town that nestles in the Lebanon Valley. Founded in 1903 by Milton S. Hershey, it is a planned industrial community that includes the Hershey Foods Corporation, one of the world's largest chocolate and cocoa plants.

WHAT TO SEE

Founders Hall. US-322, 1.25 miles east of P-743. On the campus of the Milton Hershey School is Founders Hall, a tribute to Mr. and Mrs. Milton Hershey. A diorama presents an overview of the Hershey School program. A 26-minute film depicts the founding of the town. Free. (717) 534-3557.

Hershey Park. Located just off P-743 and US-422. See 81 acres of pure fun in the heart of chocolate country. Seven theme areas include German, English, and Pennsylvania Dutch environments. The Comet, a classic, top-rated wooden roller coaster for the serious thrill-seeker, and a full assortment of rides for all ages will challenge the visitor to do it all in one day. Fast-food from the pavilions is a cut above the fare usually found at theme parks. Don't miss the chocolate-coated walk-away sundaes! (717) 534-3916

Hershey Gardens. Park Boulevard, near Hotel Hershey. A series of six themed gardens features a beautiful array of flowers, trees, and shrubs. Garden types include colonial, Italian, Japanese, English formal, and rock. Check for local information regarding the best seasons for visiting. Fee. (717) 534-3060.

Hershey Museum of American Life. Adjacent to the Hershey Park

NORTH

entrance, off Park Avenue. The museum offers a colorful collection of Pennsylvania Dutch arts and crafts. Also represented are artifacts of the American Indian and Eskimo. Other exhibits include Pennsylvania-German folk art, musical instruments, baskets, pewter, and pottery. Fee. (717) 534-3439.

Hershey's Chocolate World. Park Boulevard at Hershey Park. Stroll up the ramp in this fun-filled building to see pictures and memorabilia depicting the birth of chocolate as a confection. Candy molds, milk cans, and package wrappers take you on a nostalgic trip to your sweet tooth's past. Hop aboard a moving cart to learn about chocolate—from its origin to its consumption. This is a truly delectable attraction. Free. (717) 534-4900.

To return home, take P-39 to US-322 west toward Harrisburg. Then take I-83 south to Baltimore.

WHERE TO EAT

Hotel Hershey. Park Boulevard across from Hershey Park. This lovely hotel is set within beautifully landscaped grounds. The spacious dining room offers a view of the gardens. The menu features American cuisine and is well prepared. If you overindulge, you may welcome some exercise on the adjacent biking and jogging trails. Entertainment may be featured. $$-$$$; ☐. (717) 533-2171.

Hershey Lodge and Convention Center. West Chocolate Avenue and University Drive in Hershey proper. This sprawling complex is ideal for groups as well as the individual traveler and features three dining rooms with varying fare. Quality is consistent. $-$$; ☐. (717) 533-3311.

NORTH

Day Trip 4

KUTZTOWN, PA.
LANCASTER, PA.

KUTZTOWN, PA.

This small Pennsylvania Dutch town was founded in 1771 by George Kutz and designated the home of Pennsylvania Dutch crafts. Visitors today can observe the various techniques employed in the local art form. The biggest happening in this town is on July 4th each year. The Kutztown Folk Festival is a well-promoted event which draws enthusiastic crowds. Featured are Pennsylvania Dutch foods, arts and crafts, quilts, square dancing, and an exhibition of the Amish Plain and Fancy Dutch pageantry.

Take I-83 north out of Baltimore to York, Pa., then US-30 east out of York to Lancaster. Pick up US-222 northeast past Reading (see Day Trip 5 in this section) and on to Kutztown.

WHERE TO GO

Crystal Cave. Two miles north of Kutztown, off US-222. The route is well marked with signs. This natural phenomenon is appropriately named for the crystalline formations found in the cavern. Fee. (215) 683-6765.

LANCASTER, PA.

Retrace your routing from Kutztown and head southwest on US-222 back to Lancaster. This town, rich with restored architectural heritage dating back to the early 1700s, lends itself well to a walking tour, and its history is also reflected in the colorful shops and restaurants that abound here.

NORTH

During the Revolutionary era it was the largest inland city in the original 13 colonies. It held the status of national capital for one day in 1777 and was the state capital from 1799 to 1812.

Lancaster is in the heart of Lancaster County, which is famous for its Amish and Mennonite people. Pennsylvania Dutch hospitality is well known for its traditional family recipes served abundantly in smorgasbord style. Have your day trip dinner in one of the many area restaurants boasting local fare. While the emphasis is on mealtime, it is also on snacktime! This area features pretzel-making at its best. A visit to a local factory is on the agenda.

Lancaster County road signs will entertain you with such destinations as Paradise, Blue Ball, Bird-in-Hand, and Intercourse.

While tourists are eagerly recruited, it behooves the visitor to read the tourism literature offered locally to avoid infractions of area customs. In some instances photography is not welcomed, so check before snapping. For this information and more, a visitor's center is located east on US-30 at 1799 Hempstead Road. An orientation to the area is presented with maps, films, and exhibits. (717) 299-8901.

WHERE TO GO

Dutch Wonderland. US-30, 4 miles east of Lancaster. This theme park features an overhead Monorail Train, which offers a birds-eye view of its various attractions and rides. Traditional park activities include the exciting Log Flume ride, Stern Wheel Riverboat, Botanical Gardens, and a miniature railroad. Fee. (717) 291-1888.

Wheatland. 1120 Marietta Avenue P-23 in Lancaster. Wheatland, the mansion residence of James Buchanan, offers the visitor a unique glimpse into the life of an American president at the middle of the 19th century. The restored Federal-style house was built in 1828. Buchanan purchased the 22-acre estate in 1848 while serving as secretary of state. At the close of Buchanan's presidency in 1861, he retired to Wheatland. Visitors can view a variety of period rooms, including the elegant American Empire dining room. Also on view are the original interior paint, grained woodwork, marble and slate mantels, columned front and rear porticoes, and other architectural details. Guided tours are available. Special Christmas candlelight tours are held in early December. Call ahead for exact dates and hours. Fee. (717) 392-8721.

Strasburg Rail Road. From Lancaster take US-222 south to P-741 and head east to Strasburg. This coal burning, steam locomotive with coal oil lamps and potbelly stove is well over half a century old. The train is in character with the rustic country through which it passes. The 150-year-old right of way of the Strasburg Rail Road winds through the very heart of Lancaster County's Amish country. If you wish, bring your picnic lunch and stop over at Groff's free Picnic Grove. Fee. (717) 687-7522.

Ephrata Cloister. From Lancaster take US-222 north to Ephrata, then go west on US-322 to Ephrata Cloister. This unique site is an 18th-century German Protestant monastic settlement in the Pennsylvania

NORTH

Dutch country. It is one of America's earliest communal societies. Housed in a unique collection of medieval-style buildings, this community of religious celibates practiced an austere lifestyle which emphasized spiritual and mystical goals rather than material objectives. Ten of the original buildings have been restored to re-create this unusual village. Fee. (717) 733-6600.

Pennsylvania Farm Museum. 2451 Kissel Hill Road (take P-272 4.5 miles northeast from Lancaster). The Pennsylvania Farm Museum is an outdoor museum of Pennsylvania's rural heritage. Clustered around the crossroads of Landis Valley, the museum consists of a collection of 22 exhibit buildings and numerous objects depicting traditional crafts, skills, and lifestyles of rural Pennsylvania from the colonial era through the end of the 19th century. Fee. (717) 569-0401.

Bird-in-Hand Farmer's Market. Located 5 miles from Lancaster on Old Philadelphia Pike (P-340) at Maple Avenue. Visit this colorful market for fresh fruits and produce, homemade baked goods, Pennsylvania Dutch pretzels and potato chips, candies, flowers and plants, seafood items, and homemade ice cream. Check for market days and hours. (717) 393-9674.

Anderson Bakeries, Inc. 2060 Old Philadelphia Pike (P-340). From Lancaster take US-30 to P-340. See pretzels being made from start to finish, and share your marvelous Lancaster munchies with folks back home. Free. (717-299-2321).

Heading back, take US-30 southwest out of Lancaster to York. Then take I-83 south to Baltimore.

WHERE TO EAT

The Family Style Restaurant and Dutch Marketplace. Take US-30, from Lancaster and drive 4.5 miles. This fun dining spot features Pennsylvania Dutch food as well as a gift shop, bakery, and handcrafts. The restaurant boasts that "kids pay only what they weigh" at five cents per pound! $; ☐. (717) 393-2323.

Plain and Fancy Farm and Dining Room. Seven miles east of Lancaster on US-30 in Bird-in-Hand. Family style Pennsylvania Dutch dining. Village of shops and museums. Closed Sunday. $;☐. (717) 768-8281.

Willow Valley Inn and Family Restaurant. US-222, 3 miles south of Lancaster. Delicious farm-fresh food is served in the traditional smorgasbord style. Lodging, bake and gift shops, and an enclosed mall with 20 shops make this a good multi-purpose stop. $-$$; ☐. (717)464-2711.

N O R T H

Day Trip 5

READING, PA.

Forget the history... the main event in this town is in the here and now! Welcome to Reading, the "Outlet Capital of the World." Grab your mad money for some of the best bargains you'll ever find. Plan to shop for Christmas in an area saturated with more outlets for reduced-price merchandise than you can imagine. Enough said... here's how to get there. Take I-83 north out of Baltimore to York, Pennsylvania. Pick up US-30 to Lancaster, then US-222 to Reading. For detailed maps of the area to plan a time-efficient shopping trip, write Reading-Berks County Pennsylvania Dutch Travel Association, Sheraton Berkshire Inn, US-422, Reading-Wyomissing, PA, 19610. (215) 375-4085.

WHERE TO GO

The Reading Outlet Center. 800 block of North 9th Street, bounded by Douglass, Moss, and Windsor streets. Name brand cosmetics, linens, children's wear, sweaters, lingerie, wine and cheeses, knitted goods, and shoes. (215) 373-5495.

The Great Factory Store Outlet Center. 1110 block of Moss Street. Distributor's outlet for cookware, jewelry, hosiery, luggage, handbags, and more. (215) 378-1681).

The Big Mill Factory Outlet. 8th and Oley. A wide range of shoes for men, women, and children. Also features leather goods, housewares, lingerie, and jewelry. (215) 378-9100).

Vanity Fair Outlet Complex. 8th and Hill Avenues, West Reading-Wyomissing. Wear comfortable shoes, or buy them, as you scout bargains in this outlet paradise. A full range of famous-name clothing, handbags and luggage, power tools and accessories, china and glass, and home furnishings will place a "no holds barred" on your pocketbook. (215) 378-0408.

This sample of outlets will give you an indication of what to expect in this shopper's heaven. It's so extensive it can be bewildering, so write ahead for information. Reverse routing will bring you easily back to Baltimore.

NORTH

WHERE TO EAT

Mill Acres Restaurant and Cafe. 1295 Pennsylvania Avenue (US-422 west) near the Vanity Fair Complex. For eating in or take-out, this restaurant features specialties with home-baked breads and croissants. $; ☐ (215) 373-2988.

NORTHEAST

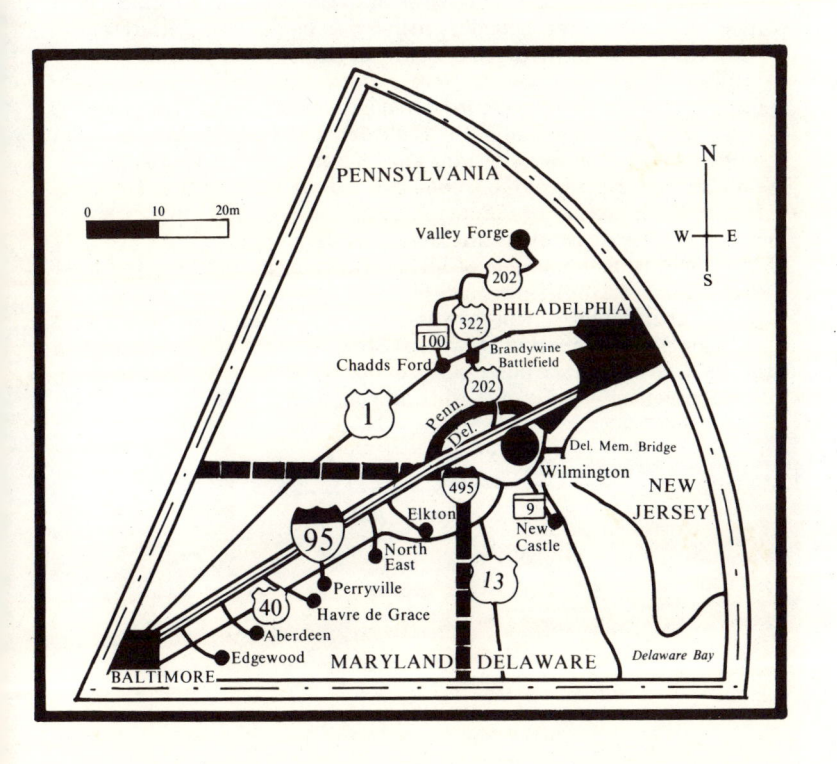

NORTHEAST

Travel northeast to the scenic blend of rolling farmlands and the upper Chesapeake Bay countryside. Historic paths yield glimpses of early American stone homes and mills and fields of grazing thoroughbreds. The headwaters of the bay challenge residents and visitors to the active arts of sailing and boating. Even the spectator sportsman will thrill to a vicarious voyage while overlooking the bay from "the decks" of a well-placed lawn chair.

Spanish Jesuit missionaries visited these shores as early as 1570. Capt. John Smith came here in 1608 during his visits to the head of the Chesapeake Bay and the Susquehanna River. A petition from the Upper Bay citizens in 1773 established Harford as a separate county. On March 22, 1775, in the Harford County seat of Bushtown, 34 prominent men penned their signatures to what is believed to be the first Declaration of Independence ever made in America by an elected body of men.

While early political events were carving a niche in history, early transportation was carving a route through the countryside. The northeast corridor saw the completion of the Baltimore and Ohio Railroad early in the 19th century. The Susquehanna and Tidewater Canal opened in 1839. We'll visit historic tributes to these land-and-sea feats on this day trip.

Rural life was touched by the encroaching industries of the iron furnaces, forges, and mills. Remaining structures show the architecture and artifacts of the times, while a museum of history provides a window to the rural household and way of life.

Our northeast journey will take us over the Maryland line, where we'll see a sample of neighboring Delaware. Philadelphia will be a day trip in itself. And, finally, at the outer limits of our two-hour drive, we'll venture into the green, easy living of the historic and scenic Brandywine Valley.

Grand Staircase at Winterthur Museum and Gardens

NORTHEAST

Day Trip 1

EDGEWOOD, MD.
ABERDEEN, MD.
HAVRE DE GRACE, MD.
PERRYVILLE, MD.
NORTH EAST, MD.
ELKTON, MD

EDGEWOOD, MD.

This day trip to the Northeast includes some stopover points worth mentioning as we proceed to the "meatier" destinations. Edgewood is a military-oriented town, which hosts the Edgewood Arsenal and the Edgewood Area of the Aberdeen Proving Ground. To see the perimeter of this complex, take I-95 north out of Baltimore to M-24 east to Edgewood.

WHERE TO GO

The Edgewood Model Railroad, Building No. E 4310, Otto and Douglas Road. Take I-95 north to M-24 east to the Edgewood Area of the Aberdeen Proving Ground. This attraction boasts one of the oldest model railroad displays in the country. Eight miniature HO (designated size) scale trains travel over a 1300-foot network of track through simulated flatlands and colorful mountains. (The model railroad may move to another building, so the curator recommends checking ahead for accurate information.) Free. (301) 676-9323.

NORTHEAST

ABERDEEN, MD.

Like Edgewood, this quiet county town is military-oriented and is the home of many of the civilian employees of the nearby Proving Ground. It hosts the U.S. Army Ordnance Museum—a site of considerable value to visitors interested in the history of military weaponry. Continue on I-95 north to M-22 and head east to Aberdeen.

WHERE TO GO

Aberdeen Proving Ground, From Aberdeen, continue on M-22 east to the entrance of the Proving Ground. This road is also known as the Aberdeen Thruway and becomes the Northern Thruway as it enters the Proving Ground. Pick up your visitor information at the main gate of this 80,000-acre reservation. Constructed in 1917, it was used for the development and testing of artillery. A display of U.S. tanks at the entrance of the grounds includes models beginning with 1918.

The U.S. Army Ordnance Museum. Located on the property of the Aberdeen Proving Grounds, this museum presents the most comprehensive collection of small arms, artillery, combat vehicles, and ammunition in the country. Among the items on display are body armor, uniforms, weapons of historic importance (Gatling Gun and German V2 Rocket), General Pershing's Locomobile, and the "Tank Park," featuring an array of vehicles ranging from World War I to the present. Free. (301) 278-3602.

HAVRE DE GRACE, MD.

This delightfully scenic town was settled before the Revolutionary War. Located at the headwaters of the Chesapeake Bay where it meets the Susquehanna River, its history is a rich one. The town enjoyed significant commerce in coal, lumber, grain, ore, and iron products through its canal between Havre de Grace and Pennsylvania. In 1836 a railroad and a steamship line were added. While the War of 1812 devastated many of its buildings, some examples of the architectural styles erected by the wealthy merchants of the 1800s remain and are maintained as homes or offices today. The current City Hall on Union Avenue was once a three-story opera house and was damaged by fire in 1920. It was later reconstructed as the present two-story building. Take I-95 north to M-155 east to Havre de Grace.

NORTHEAST

WHERE TO GO

Havre de Grace City Park. Commerce Street and Union Avenue. This peaceful plot of green marks the spot where British troops landed in 1813 to sack and burn the town. The **John O'Neill Monument** and a citizens monument to the memory of all the soldiers who fought in World War I are located here.

The Concord Point Lighthouse. Lafayette Street near Tydings Memorial Park. Considered among the oldest of such structures on the east coast, the lighthouse was erected in 1829 and was continuously operated until 1976. It offers today's visitors a magnificent view of the Bay. Free. (301) 939-1800.

The Susquehanna Museum Lock House. Erie Street. The museum is situated at the remains of the first lock of the Susquehanna and Tidewater Canal. It is furnished in the manner of an 1840 lock house. Free. (301) 939-1800.

Rock Run Mill. From Havre de Grace take M-155 west to Lapidum Road, crossing over I-95. At Lapidum Road turn right. Take this directly into Susquehanna State Park (see listings at back of book). This stone mill was built in 1794 and boasts a 12-ton water wheel, which still grinds corn today. This area was a major crossroads from Philadelphia during the 19th century. Also on the park grounds is the **Jersey Toll House** (c. 1818), which was the residence of the toll keeper for Rock Run. Currently it houses mementos of the past and a diorama of the Rock Run area of the 1850s. Free. (301) 939-0643.

The Steppingstone Museum. 463 Quaker Bottom Road. Susquehanna State Park (see listing in back of book). Surrounded by barns and other farm buildings, this stone farm house contains exhibits and displays of rural "Americana" between 1880 and 1910. The farm house is arranged as a country house with rear terrace overlooking the Susquehanna River. The tools of a woodworker, leather worker, blacksmith, and other artisans are on display. Fee. (301) 939-2299.

WHERE TO EAT

The Bayou Restaurant. 927 Pulaski Highway (US-40). Located in Havre de Grace it offers a well-rounded menu of American cuisine and excellent lunches. $-$$; ▢. (301) 939-3565.

The Bay Steamer. At the foot of Franklin Street in Havre de Grace. Located on the water, this favorite dining spot features a good seafood selection. $$; ▢. (301) 939-3626.

PERRYVILLE, MD.

Perryville is located in Cecil County near the top of the Chesapeake Bay.

NORTHEAST

It is well placed in an area of gently rolling hills and scenic rivers. Various mansions, taverns, mills, and inns easily take the visitor back to colonial times. Drive out of Havre de Grace on US-40 north across the Susquehanna Toll Bridge. Take M-222 southeast to M-7 and then northeast to Perryville.

WHERE TO GO

Rodgers Tavern. Located by the river at the Pennsylvania Railroad Bridge, about 1 mile off US-40. The existence of this charming, three-story structure was first documented in the late 1600s as a place for refreshment along the Post Road. It was acquired in 1780 by John Rodgers, father of Commodore John Rodgers—a naval hero of the War of 1812. Famous visitors to this inn included George and Martha Washington, the Marquis de Lafayette, and James Madison. Open for tours. Free. (301) 642-6066.

Principio Furnace. Continue on M-7 east for about 2 miles. In the scenic, wooded valley surrounding Principio Creek, lie the remains of the historic Principio Furnace. These iron works, the first in the British Colonies, were built in 1715 and made ammunition and cannons for the Revolutionary armies. During the War of 1812, the furnace was destroyed. In 1829 a new furnace was built near the site of the original and continued to function until early in the 20th century. While this place is primarily a "drive-by" during most of the year, the Christmas season here features a festive, outdoor market of outstanding seasonal decorations. Free. (301) 398-0200, Ext. 144.

NORTH EAST, MD.

Settlement in this area seems to have originally centered on a flour mill erected here in 1716. Also in operation here was a forge erected around 1735 by the Principio Company. The buildings in existence today are largely from the late 19th and early 20th centuries. Several small cottage industries are sustained by this community today. Continue on M-7 northeast to North East.

WHERE TO GO

St. Mary Anne's Protestant Episcopal Church. South Main Street (M-272). Erected in 1742, this church is one of the oldest in Cecil County. The structure is gambrel-roofed with clipped gables and round-headed windows. The brick is laid in Flemish bond style. The cornerstone bears the initials of the rector and vestrymen. A bible, communion vessels, and a book of common prayer presented by the Queen of England are still used in special services. The graveyard contains the markers of some American Indian converts. Fee. Open daily; no phone.

The Upper Bay Maritime Museum. In North East, take M-272 south to Walnut Street. Turn right and proceed to the North East

NORTHEAST

Community Park. This exhibit brings the taste and history of the upper Chesapeake Bay to its visitors. Fishing, boating, and hunting artifacts, native to this area, are on display. Donations accepted. (301) 287-5718.

ELKTON, MD.

This county seat was known in colonial days as "Head of Elk." It occupies an important page in American history as the point where troops and supplies of both armies were shifted from time to time during the Revolutionary War. At **Hollingsworth Tavern** on Main Street, the commanding British general, Lord Howe, may not have been impressed that, on the previous night, Gen. George Washington had slept in the very room prepared for Howe.

The town is noted as an early shipping point for the wheat raised in the rich Piedmont area. Surrounding creeks supplied the water power for small paper and textile factories which were built in the early 19th century.

Perhaps one of its most unique "industries" was the lucrative business of marrying couples who were unwilling to wait the time required in surrounding states. While a 48-hour waiting period was finally adopted in 1938 by Maryland, the town still has its wedding chapels and remains a popular place for elopements. Depart North East on M-272 north to US-40 to Elkton.

WHERE TO GO

The Cecil County Library. 135 E. Main Street. The library is located in an old home indicative of the dignity and elegance of the past periods. On the second floor is a museum of local antiquities maintained by the county Historical Society. Free. (301) 398-0914.

The Mitchell House. Located next to the library, it was built in 1769 and was the home of Dr. Abraham Mitchell, a noted physician. It served as a hospital for wounded Continental soldiers who were under Dr. Mitchell's care during the Revolution. The structure is of stuccoed brick and is maintained as a private home (drive by only).

Mount Harmon. From Elkton take M-213 south to M-282 west and follow the signs. This 18th-century tobacco plantation features a restored mansion, beautiful grounds, and formal boxwood gardens. It rests elegantly on the shores of the Sassafras River and is open for tours from April through October. Fee. (301) 275-2721.

NORTHEAST

Day Trip 2

WILMINGTON, DE.
NEW CASTLE, DE.

WILMINGTON, DE.

"Chemical Capital of the World" as well as industrial and shipping hub, Wilmington has established itself as the largest city in Delaware. It was initially known as Fort Christina in 1638 and later re-named when wealthy Quakers laid out the present town in 1731. It grew into an important market and shipping center, assisted by its accessibility to other Eastern ports and the abundant waterpower in the Brandywine River Valley.

A major benefactor arrived on the scene in the early 19th century. Eleuthere du Pont de Nemours established a high-quality gunpowder manufacturing industry here and was instrumental in bringing to this city the leading industrial status it enjoys today. The Du Pont Corporation has grown to be one of the largest industrial establishments in the world.

From Baltimore you can take I-95 directly to Wilmington, or take your time and wend your way along the route proposed in Day Trip 1 of this sector.

WHERE TO GO

Lady Christina. 100 King Street. From I-95 north, take Exit 6 (Wilmington Boulevard) into Wilmington. Follow Wilmington Boulevard to King Street, ½ block from the railroad station.

Daily, year-round lunch and dinner cruises on the Christina River are offered aboard the *Lady Christina*, a 350-passenger, climate-controlled pleasure vessel. Two enclosed decks have comfortable dining rooms, hot buffets, and a musical revue. The open, third deck is great for viewing the river at "see" level. Reservations recommended. Fee. (302) 658-4522.

The Hagley Museum. From I-95 north in Wilmington, take P-52

NORTHEAST

northwest to P-141 east for ½ mile. The original Du Pont Company's black powder mills are now the site of the 225-acre complex of the Hagley Museum, located along the Brandywine River. It offers a unique glimpse into American industrial life in the 19th-century. The main building houses exhibits that trace America's industrial development from colonial water-powered flour mills to the giant steam-powered industries of the late 19th century. Leaving the main museum building, you will enter the powder yards where massive granite mills are a testimony to the age of water power and the powderman makes his routine rounds of demonstrations. Fee. (302) 658-2400.

The original Du Pont home, **Eleutherian Mills,** on the museum grounds, is filled with the heirlooms of five generations. A barn filled with carriages and wagons, a garden, and the surrounding grounds are open to explore. Built in 1803, this charming Georgian-style residence artfully reflects the tastes of the family and the era. It is located ¼ mile from the main exhibit building and may be reached by a small bus. (Same fee and phone as above).

Old Town Hall. 512 Market Street Mall in Wilmington. Built between 1798 and 1800, Old Town Hall functioned as a center of political and social activities during the height of Wilmington's mercantile-milling economy. This Georgian-style structure housed the city's meeting chambers, offices, and jail, as well as headquarters for the library and civic organizations. It is now a museum featuring exhibits on Delaware's history, plus displays of the Historical Society of Delaware's regional decorative arts, paintings, and children's toys. The jail cells in the basement have been restored as a reminder of the structure's original function as a public building. Free. (302) 655-7161.

The Delaware Art Museum. 2301 Kentmere Parkway in Wilmington. Take P-52 north off I-95 to the museum, which houses one of the country's finest collections of American paintings, sculptures, photographs, and crafts. Various changing exhibitions of traditional and contemporary arts plus a children's gallery for an enjoyable hands-on encounter with art, make this a valuable stop for the whole family. Free. (302) 571-9590.

The Grand Opera House. 818 Market Street Mall. Built by the Masons of Delaware in 1871, this fine example of cast-iron architecture is Delaware's Center for the Performing Arts. The opera house is a National Historic Landmark and featured such famous performers as Ethel Barrymore, Edwin Booth, George M. Cohan, and Buffalo Bill Cody. Live performances (fee) and special dinners and receptions are held in the elegant decor of the Victorian era. Free tours. (302) 658-7897.

Nemours Mansion Rockland Road between US-202 and P-141. The Mansion is a fine example of a modified Louis XVI chateau. Designed by Carrere and Hastings of New York, it was built between 1909 and 1910 by Smyth and Son of Wilmington for Alfred I du Pont—a member of the American manufacturing family. Containing 77 rooms, the house is furnished with fine examples of antique furniture, rare rugs, tapestries, and outstanding artwork.

NORTHEAST

The Gardens, extending a third of a mile along the main vista of the house, were influenced greatly by Mr. du Pont's many trips to Europe and are a fine example of a classic French-style design. Stringent guidelines for visitors include: visitors must be over 16 years of age and must be able to negotiate stairways; photographs are not permitted in the Mansion. Tours take a minimum of two hours. Fee. (302) 651-6912 or 573-3333.

Rockwood. 610 Shipley Road. Inspired by an English country house, this fine example of Rural Gothic architecture reflects the lifestyle of several generations of Wilmington businessmen. Built in 1851 by Joseph Shipley, a Quaker merchant, the estate passed down through his family. The museum contains decorative arts and archives ranging from the 17th to the early 20th century and includes American, European, and Oriental objects. Fee. (302) 571-7776.

Winterthur Museum and Gardens. From Wilmington take Exit 7 off of I-95 to P-52 northwest for 6 miles. This vast museum in a 963-acre country setting is the extraordinary legacy of Henry Francis du Pont. A collection of more than 70,000 objects is housed in a nine-story sprawling building set among 200 landscaped acres, rolling meadows, and untouched woods. Prepare to witness an absolutely exquisite collection of American antiques and a garden of native and exotic plants of spectacular beauty. Fee. (302) 654-1548 or 656-8591.

WHERE TO EAT

Columbus Inn, 2216 Pennsylvania Avenue. Take Exit 7 off of I-95 to P-52 northwest. American cuisine. Comfortable, Early American interior. Reservations advised. $$; ☐. (302) 571-1492.

Hotel du Pont's Brandywine and Green Room, Hotel du Pont, 11th and Market streets. Consistently good food and competent service. Ornately decorated; dress code observed. Children's menu available. $$-$$$; ☐. (302) 656-8121.

NEW CASTLE, DE.

Since 1651, New Castle has nestled on the banks of the Delaware River. Its history is as engaging as its cobblestone streets. Founded by the Dutch, conquered by the Swedes and English, and prominent as the capital of Delaware in the early Revolutionary War era, New Castle began her story when European explorers sailed up the Delaware. Many of the private, restored homes around the Green and along The Strand are especially representative of the beauty of the architecture in the area. From Wilmington take D-9 south to New Castle.

WHERE TO GO

The George Reed II House, 42 The Strand. The Historic Society of

NORTHEAST

Delaware maintains this fine example of late Georgian architecture overlooking the Delaware River. The formal garden surrounding the house was completed in 1847 and remains faithful to its original design. Fee. (302) 322-8411.

The Green, Delaware Street between Third and Market streets. This area was laid out in 1655 by Peter Stuyvesant, the Dutch colonial governor and founder of New York. It served as the center for fairs and weekly markets. It was also the High Sheriff's House, with an adjoining jail. In the jail yard, a high stone wall encloses a pillory, gallows, and whipping post. Free.

The Strand. This interesting cobblestone street near the river is charmingly bordered by shady brick walks and brick gutters. Fine townhouses that date back to 1679, survivors of the "Great Fire" of 1824, line the Strand.

The Old State Court House. Delaware Street between Third and Market streets. Erected in 1732, it served as Delaware's colonial capitol and first state house. It was restored in 1804 to the original appearance, as in a drawing by Benjamin Henry Latrobe. Free. (302) 323-4453.

The Old Dutch House. 32 N. Third Street. This house, thought to be the oldest brick house in the state, was built in the late 17th century. Restored as a museum, it displays household utensils of the early Dutch settlers. Fee. (302) 322-9168.

WHERE TO EAT

Lynnhaven Inn. 154 N. Du Pont Highway. Comfortable environment with a reasonably priced menu. $-$$; □. (302) 328-2401.

Newcastle Inn. Market Street, ½ block north of Town Hall. Quaint, colonial setting with the convenience of a children's menu. Reservations recommended for weekends. $$; □. (302) 328-1798.

NORTHEAST

Day Trip 3

PHILADELPHIA, PA.

Philadelphia is a day trip unto itself. It's a journey into the nation's past, tracing the footsteps of George Washington, Benjamin Franklin, and Thomas Jefferson through Independence Historical Park. Get in touch with the enthusiasm and commitment of our forefathers as you touch the Liberty Bell and stand in the room where the Declaration of Independence and the U.S. Constitution were signed.

World-class museums of art, science, and history will draw you into their quiet environs and fill your day with their wonders. The performing arts—drama, music, ballet, and opera—will easily fill out your evening. The culinary arts are practiced in a virtual "restaurant renaissance" known globe-wide for fine quality. While at least one visit to Old Bookbinder's Restaurant is a must, many Philadelphia restaurants boast more personalized service and excellent food. And, if you plan to stay overnight, be sure to sample the many opportunities for nightlife—Philadelphia style.

Philadelphia is also a day trip into the present. It is a beautiful city in touch with the times. Clean, tastefully forested streets border city blocks of impressive buildings. Fine shops and fun shops offer the visitor unending opportunities to make just the right purchase. It's friendly and logically designed, making it excellent for a walking tour.

Whatever your interests might be as you approach Philadelphia for your day trip, your first stop should be the **Visitor Center** at Third and Chestnut streets in the heart of the historic district. Here you can learn about daily programs and activities and see the introductory film "Independence," which was directed by John Huston. Some free tickets for nearby attractions and information about facilities for the disabled and foreign language services are available at the Visitor Center.

NORTHEAST

Philadelphia offers such a wealth of sights and activities that detailed listings are impossible to include here. Suffice it to say that this wonderful destination exists within a day trip from Baltimore. Take I-95 north from Baltimore to Philadelphia.

You may find it wise to write in advance for information so that your travels will be time-efficient and focused on your specific interests. It is a big city, and a map of the area—especially the historic district—will be most helpful. Contact the Philadelphia Convention and Visitors Bureau, 3 Penn Center Plaza, Philadelphia, Pa, 19102. Tourist information: (215) 568-6599.

NORTHEAST

Day Trip 4

THE BRANDYWINE VALLEY, PA.
Worth More Time:
VALLEY FORGE NATIONAL HISTORICAL PARK, PA.

THE BRANDYWINE VALLEY, PA.

Rich with culture, the Brandywine Valley has become synonymous with "regional art." The artists and craftsmen of the area were, and are still, some of the finest in our country. Examples of their work can be found in many historic inns, antique shops, and museums dotting the valley.

A visit to this area is a step back into America's past. This charming countryside along the banks of the Brandywine River features museums, country estates, and some of our country's finest natural, historic, and artistic treasures. Take I-95 northeast to Wilmington, De., and take the US-202 north exit to the Brandywine Valley.

WHERE TO GO

Brandywine Battlefield State Park. Take US-202 north to US-1 west to Chadds Ford. Visit the Information Center here to see dioramas and audio-visual presentations depicting the story of Gen. George Washington's defeat by the British at the Battle of Brandywine in 1777. Two historic houses within the park, Washington's headquarters and the Marquis de LaFayette's quarters, show the life and times of the Revolutionary War period. Fee. (215) 459-3342.

Brandywine River Museum. Continue west on US-1 in Chadds Ford to the P-100 junction. Housed in a restored century-old grist mill are works by members of the Wyeth family and other outstanding American artists. Special focus is upon artists of the Brandywine River School. The museum is in an ideal setting, nestled on the peaceful, green banks overlooking the river. Special exhibits are held throughout the year in

NORTHEAST

addition to the regular ones. Fee. (215) 459-1900.

Hillendale Museum. Continue west on US-1 to P-52. Turn left and drive southeast to the junction of Hillendale and Hickory roads. This fascinating museum is a one-stop experience depicting the major influence of geography on the exploration of the North American Continent. Cassette players are carried by each visitor as he or she proceeds through the detailed dioramas. Globes demonstrate the process of westward expansion just as it was plotted by the early explorers. The final exhibit is a magnificently detailed terrain model of North America. Children must have completed the sixth grade to be admitted. Fee. (215) 388-7393.

Longwood Gardens. Return to P-52 from the Hillendale Museum and turn right. Drive north to US-1, turn left, and continue west to Kennett Square. This lovely horticultural showplace was developed by Pierre S. du Pont as a country estate. Longwood Gardens covers more than 700 acres of flowing lawns accented with fountains and sculpture. A four-acre indoor conservatory is open year-round. Special seasonal displays are coupled with permanent exhibits of exotic plants from around the world. A tourist information center is on the premises. Fee. (215) 388-6741.

Phillips Mushroom Place. Continue along US-1 west in Kennett Square. Designated the "World's Mushroom Capital," Phillips houses a free mushroom museum that explains the history, lore, and mystique of mushrooms through motion pictures, dioramas, slide presentations, and exhibits. Here the visitor observes growing mushrooms in all stages of their development. The adjoining **Market Place** offers a selection of imported gourmet foods with an offering of homemade soups, sandwiches, and of course, mushroom specialties. Also on the premises is the **Potted Place,** which features a variety of house plants, floral arrangements, herbs, and garden statuary. Free. (215) 388-6082.

Brandywine Vineyards and Winery. Continue west on US-1 to P-796 southeast to Jennersville. The rolling hills and lush valleys of the Brandywine Valley are reminiscent of the wine countries of Germany and Italy. With today's hybrid grape varieties and centuries of experience, wineries are most successful throughout the state. One example of such success is the operation here at the Brandywine Vineyards. Tours are available anytime during the winery hours. Free. For more information call (215) 255-4171.

Chadds Ford Winery. Continue your wine tasting tour by returning to Chadds Ford via US-1 east. The winery is located between the Brandywine Battlefield State Park and Longwood Gardens. Free tours and tastings are offered during winery hours, with retail sales on the premises. (215) 388-6221.

If your schedule permits, return routing to Baltimore may be planned via US-1 south through the scenic upper Chesapeake Bay territories of Cecil County and the beautiful farmlands of Harford County. For a more fast-track return, take US-202 south out of Chadds Ford to Wilmington, Delaware, and pick up I-95 south to Baltimore.

NORTHEAST

WORTH MORE TIME

Valley Forge National Historical Park. Take US-202/322 northeast out of Chadds Ford to Exit 2A (P-252). Also designated Valley Forge Road, this routing will take you directly to the historical park. This destination is beyond the recommended two-hour perimeter. But, its value for the buffs of American history makes it an exception.

The 2,800-acre park is the site of the famed winter encampment of Gen. George Washington and the Continental Army in the unforgiving winter of 1777-78. Restored buildings, soldiers' huts, cannon emplacements, and the natural setting help recreate the turning point of the American Revolution. Pack your bike, your picnic, or your hiking shoes to take extra advantage of this visitors' delight. Adjacent to the area are the **Washington Memorial Chapel** and **National Carillon** and the **Museum of the Valley Forge Historical Society.** Free. (215) 783-7700.

WHERE TO EAT

The Chadds Ford Inn. Junction US-1 at P-100. Enjoy the Early American atmosphere that blends so easily with this scenic area. This dining spot is in an inn that dates from 1736. The comfortable environment, coupled with well-prepared food, makes this a preferred dining stop. Children's menu available. $$; ☐. (215) 388-7361.

Old Trinity Church

SOUTHEAST

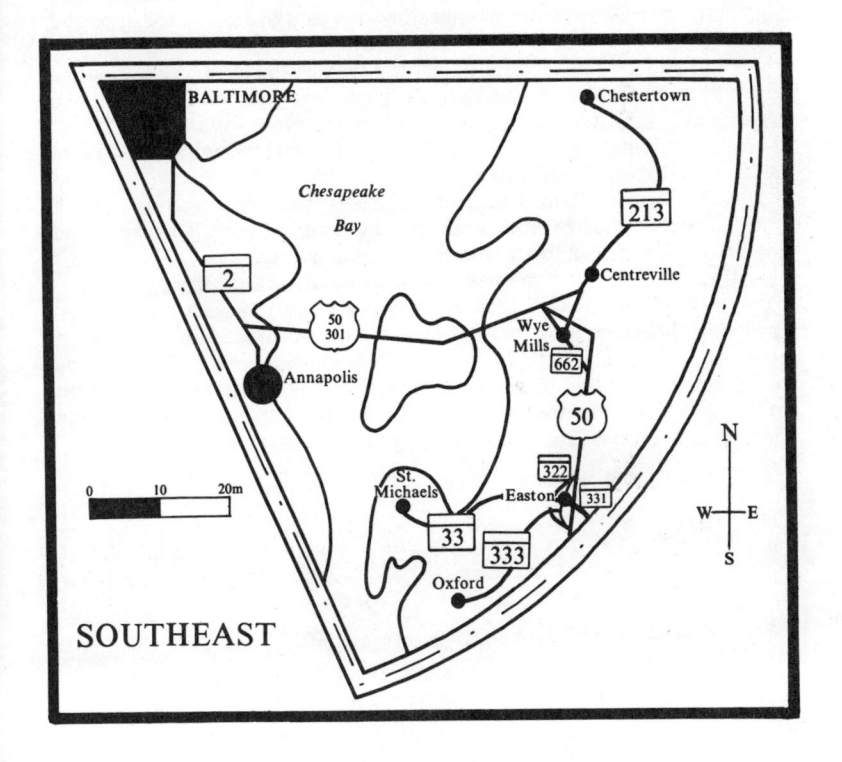

SOUTHEAST

Travel southeast to tour the heartland of Maryland's romantic and political past. Queen Anne's County was named for England's 18th-century ruler, and its courthouse at Centreville is Maryland's oldest in continuous use. Queen Anne's gives way to Talbot County and the home of the official state tree—the Wye Oak. Nearby Wye Mills was used to grind flour for Gen. Washington's troops during the American Revolution.

Maryland's Eastern Shore, where the Chesapeake Bay is a part of the scenario of life, was the setting of James A. Michener's novel **Chesapeake.** These scenic flat lands provide bike routes ad infinitum. Bikers will enjoy the easy pedaling and stimulating sights of the southeast.

In the cemeteries here headstones tell the stories of Revolutionary War patriots. You'll discover country stores and curiosity shops full of rustic souvenirs, as well as blocks of appealing homes that lead to the slips and docks harboring boats and seafood restaurants.

Oxford and St. Michaels, both historic seaport towns in Talbot County, are deeply rooted in the nation's early history. Easton, "The Colonial Capital of the Eastern Shore," is one of the cultural centers of the Shore. The annual Waterfowl Festival held here is a not-to-be-missed display of decoy carving, an indigenous art.

Beyond Easton, Oxford, and St. Michaels, the Shore is a patchwork quilt of picturesque towns surrounded by fields of corn, soybeans, and tomatoes. In summer, fresh produce stands abound on many of the area's traveling routes. Don't miss the experience of biting into a Maryland tomato. It will absolutely spoil you for pale imitations grown elsewhere. And don't husk the corn! Soak it in water and roast it in the oven or on coals for the outstanding flavor of "Silver Queen Corn." The pièce de résistance of your visit to the Shore is the fine traditional fare to be found in its proud inns and restaurants. Summer menus feature crabs and fresh fish, while in autumn and winter, oysters and clams are the catch of the day!

Hammond-Harwood House, Annapolis

SOUTHEAST

Day Trip 1

ANNAPOLIS, MD.

Don comfortable walking shoes, pack some stale bread for the ducks, and prepare to commune with history for your walking tour on the cobblestone streets of Annapolis.

Originating in 1660, Annapolis has been aptly dubbed "the museum without walls." Streets here are reminiscent of our nation's British beginnings, with names such as Duke of Gloucester, Prince George, Cornhill, King George, and Fleet. Colonial mansions and 19th-century town houses line the quaint walkways.

Annapolis was among the first American cities to develop within a pattern, rather than by chance. Consequently, the two main circles, State and Church, provide the hubs from which the secondary streets radiate. In the center of Church Circle stands **St. Anne's** with its impressive spire, and in the center of State Circle stands the **State House** of Maryland—two worthy sites to visit on the walking tour.

In the pre-Revolutionary days, Annapolis was the favorite child of the social as well as the political set. This colonial, cosmopolitan community was the center of gala parties, sporting events, balls, and theatricals. You'll see this social flair reflected in the gracious homes, renowned as some of the finest Georgian architecture in North America.

In recent years, small, neglected town houses near the City Dock have been acquired and restored by private owners. Unfortunately, above-ground wiring continues to mar the scenery at this writing. A below-ground wiring project would totally restore this lovely destination to its colonial appearance.

The town and the harbor have treated each other well over the centuries. A mutual respect is evident. The commerce that water brings is cultivated like a prime crop. The fruits of the Chesapeake Bay are offered fresh from bushel baskets or prepared from traditional recipes. Pleasure crafts dot the harbor and slip in and out of manicured marinas. The Spa Creek

SOUTHEAST

drawbridge goes up to allow these white beauties with billowing sails to glide past.

While space does not permit detailing all there is to do in Annapolis, the following is an overview of the activities that keep most people busy on this day trip. Good shopping opportunities are everywhere! Creative pottery, crafts, home decorations, and clothing are among the choice purchases. Souvenirs abound. Several places offer excellent varieties of ice cream, and a Harbor Square shop features thick slices of fudge made right before your very eyes (and nose). The gulls, ducks, and assorted birds will keep you busy at the City Dock if you bring your bread and crackers. A water tour is also offered at the foot of City Dock.

From Baltimore take M-295 south (Baltimore-Washington Expressway) to I-695 east. Then pick up M-3 south to M-100 east. Take this to M-2 south (Gov. Ritchie Highway) to the Rowe Boulevard exit into State Circle, Annapolis.

WHERE TO GO

U.S. Naval Academy. King George Street. Established in 1845, this expansive monument to higher learning is a Registered National Historic Landmark. The campus is conducive to strolling or biking and offers a sea-wall view of the academy yawls in their tutored maneuvers. "Mother Bancroft" is the name lovingly given to **Bancroft Hall** by the 4,200 midshipmen who dwell in this home-away-from-home. Impeccable order in the dormitory sets the standard that prevails from ship to shore.

The Naval Academy Chapel, which dominates the campus, is an impressive structure adorned with magnificent stained-glass windows and massive bronze doors. The traditional singing of the Navy Hymn, "Eternal Father Strong to Save," at the conclusion of services is an experience long remembered by visitors. Each June the Chapel becomes especially alive with June Week weddings. In the crypt beneath the chapel is the bronze and marble **Sarcophagus of John Paul Jones**, the naval hero of the American Revolution. The **USNA Museum** in Preble Hall contains paintings of naval heroes, ship models, uniforms, and naval memorabilia. The precision Dress Parades are always a treat to see. Stop in the Information Center located in Ricketts Hall for specific information and a map of the grounds. Charge for guide service only. (301) 263-6933.

Chesapeake Marine Tours. Slip 20, City Dock. Tour Annapolis with a water-view perspective. A series of tours ranging from 40 minutes to a full "Day on the Bay" offer narrated excursions complete with comforts and refreshments. Fee. (301) 268-7600.

Market House. Located at the head of City Dock, Market House is filled with stalls featuring fresh produce, fancy cheeses, breads and pastries, stand-up eating spots, and of course, fresh seafood. Bring your cooler along to take home some of this Chesapeake bounty.

Cornhill Street. From Market House, take Cornhill Street to State Circle. Along the way you'll see town houses reminiscent of the colonial era. The street boasts fine examples of restored old homes that abound

SOUTHEAST

in this historic district. Door decorations are especially delightful at Christmas-time.

Maryland State House. State Circle. Erected 1772-1779, this is the oldest state house in continuous legislative use in the nation. This Registered National Historic Landmark occupies a "picture postcard" setting atop an elevated crest. It was the national capitol between November of 1783 and August of 1784 and was the site of the ratification of the Treaty of Paris, as well as where George Washington resigned his commission as Commander-in-chief of the Continental Armies. On the surrounding grounds, visitors can see five cannons that arrived on the *Ark and the Dove* along with many original settlers in Maryland in 1634. The tiny brick **Treasury** building stands as the oldest public building in the state. An audio-visual program and guided tours are available at the State House Visitors Center. Free. (301) 269-3400.

Government House. State Circle and School Street. Built in the late 1860s and remodeled in Georgian style in 1936, this charming, three-story brick residence has been the official dwelling of Maryland's governors since 1969. An open house is offered to visitors each New Year's Day by Maryland's first family—the governor and his wife. Tours at any other time must be arranged individually. Free. (301) 269-3531.

St. Anne's Church. Church Circle. Just a short block from State Circle is St. Anne's, situated centrally in Church Circle. It is the third building to be erected on the foundation of what was Maryland's first brick church. Begun in 1700, the first church stood until just before the Revolution, when it was torn down. Remaining from this earlier edifice is the communion silver bearing the coat-of-arms of its donor, King William III, who presented the gift to the parish in 1695. Sir Robert Eden, the last colonial governor of Maryland, is buried in the church graveyard. Free. Open continuously.

Chase-Lloyd House. The corner of King George Street and Maryland Avenue. This tall, imposing residence is one of the most elegant reminders of Annapolis' colonial era. It was begun in 1769 by Judge Samuel Chase, a signer of the Declaration of Independence. Unfortunately, Judge Chase was unable to financially support its completion. In 1771 it was acquired by Col. Edward Lloyd IV, a wealthy tobacco grower. Later, Colonel Lloyd became governor of Maryland and embellished the residence with marble mantels from Italy, decorated ceilings, ornate carvings, and wrought silver door latches and hinges. Fee. (301) 263-2723.

Hammond-Harwood House. 19 Maryland Avenue. Purported to be one of the most perfect examples of fine Georgian architecture in America, this residence was designed and ornamented in 1774 by William Buckland, master craftsman. The exterior is salmon-colored brick with simple lines. The house, furnished in the style of the period, is noted for its beautiful woodwork such as the exquisitely carved shutters in the dining room. Traditional decorations add a special touch to Christmas season tours. Fee. (301) 263-2723.

St. John's College. College Avenue. Stroll under towering trees and

SOUTHEAST

around the cool, green lawns of one of America's oldest campuses. Chartered in 1784, its well-known alumni include Francis Scott Key. Standing at the center of the campus is **McDowell Hall,** which was begun in 1742 as the intended residence of Gov. Thomas Bladen. Excessive costs caused the Lower House to vote against further building, and its completion was not until 1784 when the land and the house were given to St. John's College. Today it is used as the Administrative Building.

As you stand in front of McDowell Hall, you will see the famous **Liberty Tree.** This giant tulip poplar has endured through more than 400 years of history, and an agreement was signed here between the first European settlers and the Susquehannock Indians. Also located here is the **Dr. Charles Carroll House** (c. 1724), which was moved to the campus in 1957 from Main Street. Free. (301) 263-2371.

William Paca House and Garden. 186 Prince George Street. Built in 1763, this lovely Georgian residence was the winter home of William Paca, signer of the Declaration of Independence and governor of Maryland. While the interior of the house is another fine example of the masterful work of William Buckland, the gardens are an outstanding part of this historic site. The two-acre terraced garden is a restoration of the original and features a Chinese trellis bridge, domed pavilion, and a fish-shaped pond. Tours of both house and garden are available. Fee. (301) 267-8149.

Return via State Circle to M-2 north, and follow reverse routing to Baltimore.

WHERE TO EAT

The Maryland Inn. Church Circle and Main Street. The Inn was built on a piece of ground originally set aside for the use of the Town Drummer in 1694. In the 1770s, an elegant brick house was adjoined to the Inn by Thomas Hyde, an Annapolis merchant. Today it continues to host guests and diners in its charming colonial rooms. The King of France Tavern, Treaty of Paris Dining Room, and the King's Wine Cellar offer day trip visitors hospitality, Maryland style. Traditional Maryland fare. $$; ☐. (301) 269-0990. Convenient maps of historic Annapolis are available at the Inn.

The Harbor House Restaurant. City Dock. This dining spot, opened in 1960, is a favorite for its fine food and scenic location. Seafood and beef are the mainstays of the menu, which features oysters, crabs, clams, and fish from the Chesapeake Bay as well as entrees of steak and prime rib. Children's menu available. $$; ☐. (301) 268-0771.

Chick and Ruth's Delly. 165 Main Street. In this unpretentious, popular gathering spot you'll hear conversations ranging from pastrami to politics. Great sandwiches include an assortment of 26 specialties named for various politicians, such as Mayor William Donald Schaefer and Gov. Harry Hughes. $; No ☐. (301) 269-6737.

Reynolds Tavern. Church Circle and Franklin Street. Built by William Reynolds in 1737, this brick, shuttered building served as a tavern for many years and provided services to the traveler, seafarer and gentry.

SOUTHEAST

Now a marvelous colonial-style restaurant with period furnishings and decor, it also offers bed and breakfast accommodation (four suites). Continental and colonial cuisine are featured. $$; □. From Baltimore, call 269-0090. From Washington, call 261-2206. From other locations, call (301) 263-2641.

United States Naval Academy, Annapolis

SOUTHEAST

Day Trip 2

CHESTERTOWN, MD.
CENTREVILLE, MD.
WYE MILLS, MD.

CHESTERTOWN, MD.

This charming little town is situated on the banks of the peaceful Chester River and exemplifies the easy, country living of Maryland's Eastern Shore. It is renowned for its waterfront homes, built during the Revolutionary period, which can be seen from the Chester River Bridge. Georgian mansions along the water remind us of the town's history, rooted in the Revolutionary era of the 1700s. Chestertown is an excellent place for a walking tour. Examples of period architecture and brick-work abound, much of it in private homes. Downtown Chestertown offers a variety of shops. From Baltimore take M-2 south to US-50-301 east across the Chesapeake Bay Bridge. Continue on US-301 to M-213 north to Chestertown.

WHERE TO GO

Geddes-Piper House. Church Alley. This example of an 18th-century Philadelphia town house is open to the public. It is a handsome, three-story brick house built between 1730 and 1754. Currently occupied by the Kent County Historical Society, it houses a collection of old maps and 18th-century furniture. Fee. (301) 778-2623.

Walking Tours. Chestertown. Additional information on the historic houses and walking tours can be obtained from the Historical Society at (301) 778-1314 and from the Kent County Chamber of Commerce, (301) 778-0416.

SOUTHEAST

CENTREVILLE, MD.

Centreville was established around the **Queen Anne's County Courthouse,** one of the two 18th-century courthouses in existence in Maryland today. The courthouse has remained in use continuously since 1792. Located at 120 N. Commerce Street, the building of white-painted brick contrasts with the greens of the boxwood hedge and the tree-shaded square. The masonry is laid in the Flemish bond design. A large **Statue of Queen Anne,** by Elizabeth Gordon Chandler, stands on the courthouse green. From Chestertown, take M-213 south to Centreville.

WHERE TO GO

Wright's Chance. 119 S. Commerce Street. This 1740 plantation house was relocated to Centreville within walking distance from the courthouse. It features the original wood paneling and glass window panes. It now houses a museum and the headquarters for the county historical society. It is furnished in the style of the period. Fee. (301) 758-1347.

Tucker House. 124 S. Commerce Street. This is the "working museum" of the Queen Anne's County Historical Society. Guided tours available. Fee. For information regarding the properties of the historical society call (301) 758-1347.

WYE MILLS, MD

Continue your driving day trip to the town that is centered around the **Old Wye Mill.** These peaceful flatlands of the Eastern Shore provided the setting for the plantation homes of famous Maryland history-makers such as the Paca and Tilghman families. **Wye Hall,** located on nearby Wye Island, was destroyed in 1879 by fire. It was the mansion home of William Paca. **Wye Plantation,** originally owned by the Tilghman family, is a 17th-century structure that time has spared. Located on Wye Neck Road, the estate is now privately owned and raises purebred Angus cattle. From Centreville, take M-213 south to US-50. Drive south to the junction of M-404 and Wye Mills.

WHERE TO GO

Old Wye Grist Mill. At the junction of US-50 south and M-404, turn right and drive west for about one-quarter mile to the mill. This site has maintained a mill since colonial days. Flour for the troops of George Washington was ground here and, under private ownership, it continued to function for an estimated 250 years. Be sure to stop here and walk

SOUTHEAST

around the mill. While it may not be open and functioning, it is definitely worth the visit.

Wye Oak. Continue west on M-404 to M-662 south. Near this junction, situated on 29 acres, is the country's only one-tree state forest. The tree stands close to the entrance of the park off of M-662 and is well marked. The Wye Oak is Maryland's State Tree, measures 50 feet in circumference, 95 feet in height, and is approximately 400 years old. Any fallen limbs are artistically carved into prestigious gavels, and seedlings from the tree are sold by the State Forest Service. Open year-round. Free.

Old Wye Church. Located within walking distance from the Wye Oak on M-662 is one of the oldest Episcopal churches in America. The interior of this church, built in 1721, features high box pews, a hanging pulpit, a gallery bearing the Royal Arms of England and original communion pieces dating from 1737. Nearby is the reconstructed vestry house which was erected on the original foundations and furnished in 18th-century antiques. Also located here is the parish house, built in 1957 in the 18-century style. Open mid-April through November. Services are held each Sunday at 11 A.M. Free; donations accepted. (301) 827-8853.

Old Wye Grist Mill

SOUTHEAST

Day Trip 3

EASTON, MD.
OXFORD, MD.
ST. MICHAELS, MD.
Worth More Time:
BLACKWATER NATIONAL WILDLIFE REFUGE

EASTON, MD.

The "Colonial Capital of the Eastern Shore" earned its title due to the centralization of administrative offices here for all Eastern Shore counties. Dating back to the 1700s, Easton was established around the Talbot County Courthouse. During colonial times, the village developed slowly. The **Old Quaker Meeting House** is the only building from that era. After the Revolution, however, Easton grew rapidly. Much of the reason for its expansion is its central location in relationship to neighboring counties. Easton claims the first newspaper on the Eastern Shore (1790), the first bank (1805), and the first steamboat line to Baltimore (1817).

The street plan of Easton dates back to 1785. Local streets were named by Jeremiah Banning, a Talbot County landowner. Washington Street is the principle business corridor. The corner of Washington and Goldsborough streets is the site of the **Old Frame Hotel.** Standing in its place today is a hardware store which is not to be missed. The worn and creaking floor boards, metal bins of nuts and bolts, iron skillets, and oversized soup pots all take you back to the good old days. Such a collection of venerable essentials stands in glaring defiance of today's disposable society.

Continue along Washington Street to well-maintained brick buildings, which still display some original external woodwork.

The buildings on the central square were restored to a Federal-period

SOUTHEAST

style in the 1950s, and subsequent construction in the area has kept this theme. The town is charming and lends itself well to walking and biking tours. Clothing shops display the casual look; those with a penchant for geese and mallards will find much to their taste.

Easton hosts an annual fall **Waterfowl Festival**, which showcases expert decoy carving and painting by local artists. Fall fills the area hotels with avid sportsmen seeking their share of ducks. Window displays in realtor's offices tempt visitors to retire to waterfront acreage. Pubs and restaurants offer congeniality and well-prepared seafood.

From Baltimore take M-2 south to US-50-301 east, and cross the Chesapeake Bay Bridge. Follow US-50 south to M-331 west to Easton. Or, if you are coming from Wye Mills (Day Trip 2, this sector) simply follow the same route south on US-50.

WHERE TO GO

The Historical Society of Talbot County. 29 S. Washington Street. The Society is located in the **Stevens House**, a restored building built around 1800. The Federal town house is now a museum featuring period furnishings, a garden, and rotating exhibits. Fee. (301) 822-0773.

The Third Haven Quaker Meeting House. South on Washington Street past Brookletts Avenue, several blocks south of the historical society. This house is believed to be the oldest frame building dedicated to religious meetings in America. William Penn preached here, and Lord Baltimore attended the services here. Erected in 1682, the clapboard structure still contains the original broadplank floors and straightbacked benches. While not routinely open for tours, it is definitely worth walking around for a view of one of our country's earliest shrines to religious freedom. Free. (301) 822-0293.

The Academy of the Arts. Harrison and South streets. Here you can view a variety of works by local artists. (301) 822-0455.

Guided Tours of Easton. Arrangements for special guided tours (fee) of the area can be made by calling (301) 822-0773.

WHERE TO EAT

The Tidewater Inn. Dover and Harrison streets. Traditional decor with a fine Maryland kitchen. Consistently well-prepared food is served here with Eastern Shore hospitality. If you choose this as an overnight resting spot, reservations are recommended. $$; □. (301) 822-1300.

OXFORD, MD.

Early records document Oxford's existence in 1668. Situated on the Tred Avon River, the town flourished in export trading and was rivaled only by the port of Annapolis. Oxford was overshadowed by the bustling growth of Baltimore and slipped into a decline. After the Civil War, however,

SOUTHEAST

shipbuilding, oystering, and fishpacking revived the town's economy, which has remained stable ever since.

Despite its early beginning, Oxford's architecture has more 19th-century design than 18th-century. The city has remained relatively untouched by tasteless commercialism and signs. Peaceful, well-maintained homes sit like gems on green velvet cushions. Stroll through side streets and coves to small docks berthing privately owned sailcraft. Grab a taste of the Chesapeake Bay from one of the several casual and carry-out seafood kitchens located here. And see The Strand, an impressive block of homes of variable architecture propitiously placed along the Tred Avon River. A small, but delightful beach lines the bank of the Tred Avon. Local residents bring their picnic hampers and spread blankets for a summer retreat here.

The shops in Oxford are not as sophisticated as in Easton; they offer interesting bargains in a country store setting. The public park offers a pleasing access to the quiet beauty of the Tred Avon River.

In Easton, drive south on Washington Street to Peach Blossom Road (M-333). Drive south on M-333 directly into Oxford.

WHERE TO GO

The Oxford Cemetery. Located on M-333 just outside the town of Oxford is the historic Oxford Cemetery. Headstones and gravemarkers quietly understate the magnitude of the contributions to Maryland history made by those buried here. Among the most famous buried here are Col. Tench Tilghman (1744-86) and his wife, Anna Maria. Colonel Tilghman became a wealthy merchant before the outbreak of the Revolutionary War. His support of the independence movement caused great family strain, for his father was a loyalist. Tilghman served General Washington as his secretary and then as his aide-de-camp. When the victory at Yorktown was secured, it was Tilghman who carried the news of Cornwallis's surrender to Congress in Philadelphia. Descendants erected the **Tench Tilghman Monument** here in commemoration.

The Morris House. Morris Street and The Strand. Built c. 1710, this structure is part of the charming **Robert Morris Inn.** Architecturally, it is a tribute to the style of the 18th-century. In 1730, an English trading company bought the house as a residence for Robert Morris, a representative of the Oxford firm's shipping interests. Robert, Jr., his son, came from England in 1747 to join him and went on to be a signer of the Declaration of Independence and a noted financier of the Continental Army. Original floorings, mural wall coverings, and careful restoration add to the flavor of this favorite inn and dining spot. (301) 226-5111.

The Academy (Bratt) House. Several doors up from The Strand on Morris Street is the distinctive gray clapboard building that served as part of the Maryland Military School, established in 1848. A box garden now exists where the main house stood before it was destroyed by fire in 1855. The remaining landmark has a pilastered facade and cupola atop a low hipped roof. The box hedge and the wrought-iron front porch also remain. Private.

The Oxford-Bellevue Ferry. M-333 at the Tred Avon River. Also known as the **Tred Avon Ferry,** it is believed to be the oldest "free running" (not attached to a cable) ferry in the country. Initiated in 1683, it was oar-propelled until 1886 when power service began. Take a break from the road, place your car on the ferry, and connect to Bellevue on your way to St. Michaels. (301) 226-5408.

WHERE TO EAT

The Robert Morris Inn. Morris Street and The Strand. This elegant high spot of the Eastern Shore is dedicated to a tradition of quality, with consistently good food and excellent service. The Inn is featured in such publications as *Classic Country Inns of America* and *America's Historic Inns and Taverns.* Magazines such as *Southern Living, Good Housekeeping, Town and Country,* and *Better Homes and Gardens* have recommended it in their reviews.

Reservations are not accepted, as guests are served on a first-come, first-served basis. Both the Inn and the Restaurant have a quiet, conservative atmosphere. The proprietors do not welcome children under age 10 or large groups. With that in mind, if it still meets your criteria, do plan to stay the night here. Excellence prevails in the guest rooms, also, where tasteful period furnishings give you a sense of visiting the past. Accommodations range from the modestly priced singles with shared baths, to the more substantially priced combinations of bedroom and sitting room.

The Inn is open daily for dining and lodging, except Christmas holidays. In the Tap Room, casual dress is acceptable. In the Dining Room, coats are required for men, except from Memorial Day through Labor Day. $$-$$$; ☐. (301) 226-5111.

ST. MICHAELS, MD.

The unspoiled heritage of St. Michaels is reminiscent of the same economic growth, decline, and re-stabilization experienced by its neighbor, Oxford. Accessible by water on two sides and once heavily timbered, St. Michaels became a center for ship building and prosperity. The industry rose to prominence during the Revolutionary War, but declined around 1830 as a result of diminishing timber and the rise of Baltimore as a major competitor. The industry was somewhat revived in the following decade, and the seafood and agricultural processing businesses now sustain this modest town. A yachting haven, St. Michaels hosts a very popular sailing regatta in August of each year on the Miles River west of the town.

Biking is especially good in St. Michaels, as in Oxford and Easton, due to the quiet, level streets. Biking also affords a sense of closer contact with the roadside sights and quaint shops. Some of the antique shops

SOUTHEAST

here are for the more serious collector, but many are a fascinating hodgepodge of memorabilia and Americana. These colorful caches are definitely worth a visit. Depart on the Tred Avon Ferry and pick up M-329 west to M-33 west directly into St. Michaels.

WHERE TO GO

St. Mary's Square Museum. "The Green," located between Talbot and Mulberry streets. This museum of local memorabilia is located on a plot of ground around which St. Michaels was built. Fee. (301) 745-9561.

Chesapeake Bay Maritime Museum. In St. Michaels, turn right at Mill Street. The Maritime Museum is located on a peninsula in the harbor of St. Michaels. It features the Hooper Straight Lighthouse, indigenous sailing craft, maritime exhibits, a boat building workshop, and a special display of carved waterfowl. (Fee). Self-guided walking tours of St. Michaels can also be obtained here. (301) 745-2916. Return via US-50 north and follow reverse routing to Baltimore.

WORTH MORE TIME

Blackwater National Wildlife Refuge. From St. Michaels take US-50 south to M-16 southwest. Then take M-335 south along the well-signed route. Each year, thousands of migrating birds fly south to the warmer marshlands of Maryland's Eastern Shore. Wintering Canada geese flock to this refuge during November and December. Tourists can observe this natural phenomenon from driving paths that link the fields and streams. Bring your camera to "capture" the other wildlife in this refuge as well. Climb the ranger's tower to view the masses of birds and listen to their soulful honking. This destination is slightly beyond the two-hour limitations. Plan to see it, if you have the time, or if you plan to stay overnight on the Eastern Shore. A visitor's center on the refuge provides interpretive material and maps of trails and roads. Free. (301) 228-2677.

Old Trinity Church. M-16 at Church Street. While enroute to Blackwater Wildlife Refuge, you'll pass the oldest church in the country that is still in use. The church was established in 1675, and the adjoining graveyard is the resting place for many famous Marylanders. (301) 228-3999.

WHERE TO EAT

St. Michaels Inn. St. Michaels. The excellent menu features continental cuisine along with traditional seafood selections. "Bed and Breakfast" accommodations are available. $$; □. (301) 745-3303.

The Crab Claw Restaurant. Navy Point, St. Michaels, beside the Maritime Museum. Dock your boat here or park your car. In either event, don't miss the superb steamed crabs and other dishes that have made the Crab Claw the favorite dining spot of the Eastern Shore. Friendly service

SOUTHEAST

and a panoramic view of St. Michaels Harbor will cap your Maryland memories. $-$$; ☐. (301) 745-2900. Check for seasonal hours.

Chesapeake Bay Maritime Museum, St. Michaels

SOUTH

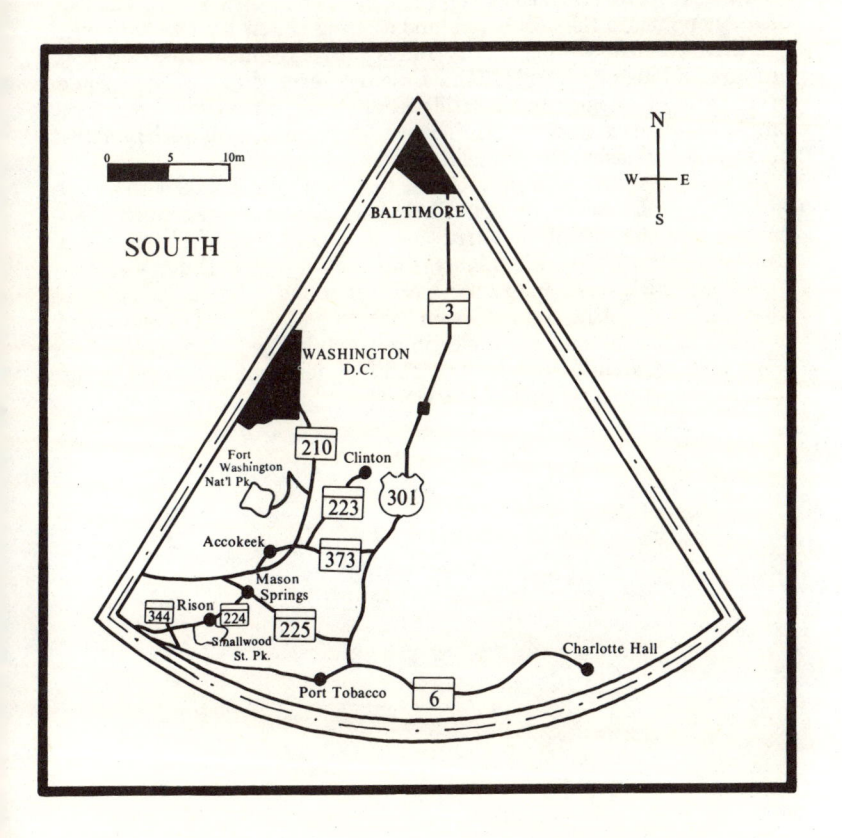

SOUTH

Our next day trip destination is in southern Maryland, where extensive plantations were a testimony to social and economic achievements. Large landowners thrived on the increasing demand for tobacco—both locally and in exports. Livestock and non-tobacco crops such as corn and wheat were also grown in these self-sustaining communities. Overwhelmingly rural, southern Maryland did not play an active part in the Revolutionary War. The area's agricultural lifestyle was largely untouched by the volatile times. Fertile soil and navigable waterways lent themselves well to tobacco production. As independent landowners prospered, their wealth was frequently applied to the acquisition and clearing of new land for farming.

A drive through southern Maryland is a drive through three centuries of Maryland history. The National Colonial Farm Museum pays tribute to the agricultural heritage that still predominates in the region. Roadside farmers' markets attest to that, offering a tempting array of fresh produce, home-baked items, preserves, jellies, and local crafts.

In Prince George's County, recorded history began in 1608 with a visit from Capt. John Smith. Active efforts here have preserved much of its heritage for the visitor of today, and it is said that you'll see more 18th-century architecture in this area than in all of Williamsburg, Virginia.

Modern "high tech" industries have also found a home in southern Maryland. Pioneering companies embark on research and development in solar cell production, micro-electronics, and biomedical research.

Agriculture, architecture, history, and high tech—all are found in the surprising southern reaches of Maryland.

Jousting—the state sport

SOUTH

Day Trip 1

PORT TOBACCO, MD.
CHARLOTTE HALL, MD.
SMALLWOOD STATE PARK, MD.

PORT TOBACCO, MD.

The quiet remains of this town mark one of the oldest inhabited sites in the United States. It was an Indian village long before Capt. John Smith explored the Potomac. Later, settled by Maryland colonists, it became an important tobacco port. From 1727 to 1895 it served as the county seat of Charles County.

In 1774 local citizens met to add their support to the growing protest against the Boston Port Act. They agreed to break off trade with Britain and to appoint delegates to the First Continental Congress. Through the efforts of William Smallwood and others, Port Tobacco became the center for Charles County's Revolutionary activities.

By 1775, the Port Tobacco Creek began to diminish, a result of silt deposits. This was the beginning of the decline of its importance as a port. That decline was hastened when the railroads by-passed it. The final blow came when Port Tobacco turned over the county seat to La Plata in 1895.

Today, in the town square, visitors can still drink from a cool spring that once supplied water to Capt. John Smith. A number of early religious landmarks are located in the vicinity. The homes of several Revolutionary patriots still exist, primarily as private residences. Two such examples on the town square are **Stagg Hall** (c. 1732) and **Chimney House** (c. 1765). From Baltimore take M-3 south to US-301 south. Then take M-6 southwest (near La Plata) to Port Tobacco.

WHERE TO GO

The Charles County Museum. Off M-6, on Chapel Point Road. Located in the reconstructed 1819 **Charles County Courthouse,** this structure was restored by the Society for the Preservation of Port Tobacco. Stop here for visitor information and exhibits on tobacco growing and processing and displays of various archeological finds. Fee. (301) 934-4313.

St. Ignatius Church. From Port Tobacco, continue on Chapel Point Road south about 3 miles. This parish was begun in 1741 by Father Andrew White as a mission to the Indians. Located at Chapel Point, high above the Potomac River, this Roman Catholic Church was completed in 1798 and is the oldest active Jesuit parish in the United States. Today, as then, it commands an excellent view of the Potomac and Port Tobacco rivers. Free. Open Daily.

Tobacco Auctions. Held in La Plata, Waldorf, and Hughesville. Tobacco has been grown in Maryland for 300 years and was utilized as currency in the 18th century. Be sure to stop for a visit at one of the auctions in the area if you are there in season: They are held Monday through Thursday, from mid-March to May. Free. Call the Tri-County Council for Tourism for seasonal details. (301) 884-2144.

CHARLOTTE HALL, MD.

In 1939 a group of Amish families moved from Pennsylvania to Charlotte Hall. This land, named for Queen Charlotte of England, sold cheaply and this encouraged the Amish to seek farmland here. By 1952, about 50 Amish families were prospering in the area. Amish religious beliefs restrict the use of modern farm equipment, automobiles, and electricity. Animals pull the plows, windmills pump water, and horses pull the carriages for transportation. The buggies can be seen along the highways traveling from church to neighbor to market. From Port Tobacco, continue on M-6 east to Charlotte Hall.

WHERE TO GO

Amish Farmers Market. Charlotte Hall, junction of M-6 and M-5. This market features Amish stalls of farm-fresh produce and home-baked breads and pies. Also on site is a flea market and an antiques auction. Open year-round on Wednesdays and Saturdays. Free.

SMALLWOOD STATE PARK, MD.

Tour 405 acres of scenic Charles County located on part of the tract of

SOUTH

land originally owned by Gen. William Smallwood. Smallwood commanded the famous "Maryland Line"—the courageous troops who covered the retreat of Washington's men at the Battle of Long Island in 1776. Their bravery earned them Washington's favor, and thereafter, Maryland was known as the "Old Line State."

Smallwood went on to become a brigadier general in 1776 and major general in 1780. He was elected to Congress and also served as governor of Maryland from 1785 to 1788. The park is open daily from 10 A.M. to 6 P.M. From Charlotte Hall, take M-6 west through La Plata and Port Tobacco to Doncaster. Pick up M-344 west to M-224 northeast into Rison and Smallwood State Park.

WHERE TO GO

Smallwood's Retreat. Smallwood State Park. This authentic restoration was completed by the Smallwood Foundation and the state of Maryland. The one-and-a-half-story, brick colonial structure with detached frame kitchen was the home of Gen. William Smallwood, a Revolutionary War hero. A colonial-style herb garden has been replanted on the grounds. Open daily from June through September, and costumed hostesses give tours during these months. Picnic areas and playgrounds are open year-round. Free. (301) 743-7613.

Old Durham Church. From Smallwood State Park, take M-224 southwest to M-344 east into Doncaster. Pick up M-6 east to M-425. Turn right and drive southwest for 1.2 miles on M-425. The modest two-story brick building will first be seen through surrounding woods. It was erected in 1732 as an early Episcopal church. General Smallwood served on its vestry for 16 years. George Washington occasionally attended services here. Among its historic contents are a silver chalice and paten dating from 1707. The Church graveyard served an even earlier congregation (two tombstones of the sons of William and Elizabeth Dent date back to 1695 and 1690). Soldiers of the Revolutionary War also are buried here. Open year-round. Free. From M-425 north pick up M-6 north to US-301 north and return to Baltimore.

If time permits retrace your path back to Smallwood State Park and take M-244 northeast to M-227. At Pomonkey take M-227 north to M-210 east and intersect M-373 northeast at Accokeek.

S O U T H

Day Trip 2

ACCOKEEK, MD.
CLINTON, MD.
FORT WASHINGTON NATIONAL PARK, MD.

ACCOKEEK, MD.

According to early documentation by Capt. John Smith, Accokeek is situated on the site of Moyanone, a Piscataway Indian village. While the village was burned in 1622, numerous artifacts have been unearthed here with the cooperation of the Smithsonian Institution. Archeological and anthropological quests have yielded thousands of skeletons, indicating that the site was occupied for several hundred years. A museum located in the public library displays some of these finds. From Baltimore take US-3 south to US-301 south. Take M-373 west, just past the M-210 junction to Accokeek.

WHERE TO GO

National Colonial Farm Museum. Bryant Point Road at the Potomac River, about 3 miles west of the M-373 and M-210 junction. Operated by the Accokeek Foundation, the museum is an example of a functioning 18th century Tidewater farm. Located on the Potomac River, it is in the central portion of Piscataway Park and commands a view of Mount Vernon, the home of the first president of the United States. It is an appropriate setting for the exhibition and demonstration of the agricultural methods, crops, livestock, and everyday living of colonial days.

Visitor information and tour arrangements can be obtained at the gatehouse. Included on the tour are the colonial crop demonstrations; an herb garden which produces more than 50 varieties used for medicinal, cosmetic, and culinary purposes; a delightful orchard, pond, and chestnut grove; and a variety of livestock typical of the times. The foundation has

SOUTH

done a very faithful job in presenting the modern-day visitor with a window to the world of the colonial era. Fee. (301) 283-2113.

CLINTON, MD.

Clinton's lure is almost entirely attributable to John and Mary Surratt. The town became known as Surrattsville when John was appointed postmaster in 1854. The family house and tavern served as a local post office, a resting place for travelers, a public dining room, and a local polling place. It was also a "safe" house for Confederate couriers.

American history enthusiasts and Abraham Lincoln "buffs" will remember it for the deeds of Mary Surratt. In 1865, Lincoln's assassin, John Wilkes Booth, and David E. Herold stopped here on the way to the home of Dr. Samuel Mudd. For her part in taking in these travelers, Mrs. Surratt was charged, found guilty, and hanged for alleged complicity in the plot to assassinate Lincoln. She was the first woman to be executed by the federal government. Controversy still prevails over her innocence, as much of the damaging testimony was unsubstantiated or extracted from unreliable sources. From Accokeek, take M-373 east to M-223 north to Clinton.

WHERE TO GO

The Surratt House. 9110 Brandywine Road. The family house, tavern, and post office were built in 1852 by John Surratt. In 1965 it was donated to the National Capital Park and Planning Commission. The property is recognized as having historic significance, and restoration was begun with the assistance of local citizens. Today visitors may tour the site (closed January and February) assisted by costumed guides and hear the intriguing details of the saga of Mary Surratt. Free; donations accepted. (301) 868-1121.

FORT WASHINGTON NATIONAL PARK, MD.

Fort Washington is an imposing example of the first fortifications erected for the defense of the Nation's Capital. George Washington selected this ideal elevated terrain along the Potomac River in 1795. While the fort erected here in 1808 commanded an excellent view of the river for miles, it was inadequate in construction and poorly planned. The British destroyed this earlier fort during the War of 1812. Maj. Charles L'Enfant, planner and designer of Washington, D.C., immediately set about constructing the present fort. A quarrel with the War Department interrupted his work and Lt. Col. Warren K. Armistead completed the construction in 1824. A visit to Fort Washington National Park is an excellent opportunity to see an example of early 19th-century strategy in defense, and garrison life.

To get here from Clinton, take M-223 southwest to where it becomes Farmington Road (just west of Piscataway). From Farmington Road, turn right on M-210 and drive north to Old Fort Road and turn left. Drive west to Fort Washington Road and turn left. Drive west to Fort Washington Park.

WHERE TO GO

Fort Washington. M-210; Silesia. One of the most interesting old military structures in the country, Fort Washington has been altered little since its construction in 1824. It is an enclosed masonry fortification entered by a drawbridge across the dry moat at the sally port. From above the main gateway you can see the entire 833-foot outline of the fort. Approximately 60 feet below the main fort is the outer V-shaped water battery, begun by Maj. Charles L'Enfant, as well as the ditch on the southwest face and most of the ditch on the northeast face. They are still in an excellent state of preservation. A double stairway connects the parade ground with a tunnel leading to the lower construction.

Two half-bastions overlook and command the river above and below the fort. Below the ramparts of these two structures are the gun positions. From these levels (water battery, casemate positions, and ramparts), guns could deliver a devastating fire against an enemy fleet on the Potomac.

The front of the structure, built of solid stone and brick masonry, is about seven feet thick. On the parade ground are the officers' quarters and the soldiers' barracks. Flanking each of these structures is a magazine. A guardroom, containing two narrow cells, and the office of the commanding officer are in the main gateway structure. Civil War weapons and garrison life demonstrations are regularly scheduled. Free. For details, call (301) 292-2112.

From Fort Washington, the most time-efficient approach to Baltimore begins with re-routing on Fort Washington Road east to M-210 north. Pick up I-95 south around the southeast perimeter of Washington to exit 22 and the Baltimore-Washington Parkway (M-295 northeast) into Baltimore.

Cherry blossom time at the Washington Monument

SOUTHWEST
And Washington
Region

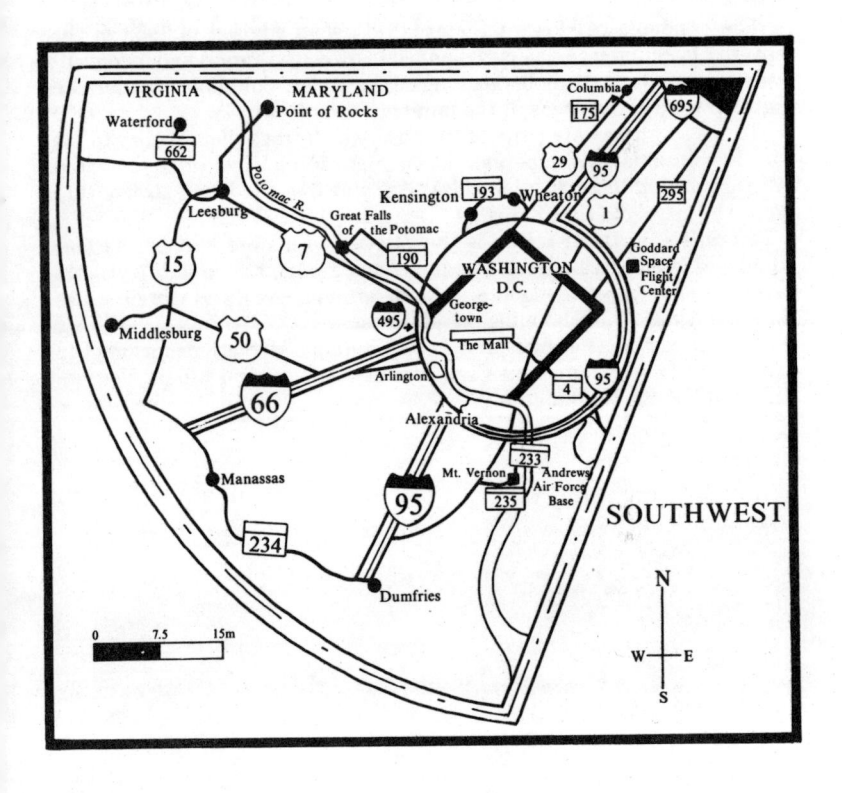

SOUTHWEST AND WASHINGTON REGION

Travel southwest to a blend of past, present, and future ... the old and historic coupled with the community of today and tomorrow. From beltway to backroads we'll take a day trip through two of America's earliest states—Maryland and Virginia—and to our nation's capital.

Rural peace and small town quiet prevailed in this area throughout the 19th century. Today, one-third of Montgomery County, Md., is residential or commercial; one-third is preserved for agricultural land; and the remainder is dedicated to open space, including more than 25,000 acres of park land. This area is unique in its beauty and its location. Easy access is afforded by major interstate highways and the Baltimore-Washington Parkway.

The residents of Howard County, Md., were advised in 1963 of the advent of Columbia, a new city planned to avoid the sprawl and inconveniences common to many burgeoning cities. Today, Columbia continues to develop toward the needs of the family of tomorrow.

To the southwest are cities of the past, which trace their history to the pre-Revolutionary War period. These historic districts offer preserved Victorian architecture, brick sidewalks, and tree-shadowed streets that keep the citys' old flavor alive.

Virginia's northern region is the gateway to a state that boasts four centuries of American development and achievement. The state's visitors are treated to majestic mountains, underground caves, and vibrant cities offering a variety of shopping possibilities.

Rich in historic treasures, northern Virginia's attractions include Old Town Alexandria, numerous Civil War battlefields, and Mount Vernon, home of George Washington.

U.S. Capitol Building, Washington, D.C.

SOUTHWEST
And Washington Region

Day Trip 1

KENSINGTON, MD.
WHEATON, MD
COLUMBIA, MD.

KENSINGTON, MD.

Kensington begins a day trip of fascinating stops. You'll pass through Howard County and rub shoulders with Columbia, a town that offers shopping and browsing.

From Baltimore take I-95 southwest toward Washington. At M-175 drive west to Columbia. Then, pick up US-29 south, which offers time-efficient and scenic routing through Howard and Montgomery counties. From US-29 south take I-495 west to Exit 33 toward Kensington.

WHERE TO GO

Mormon Temple. 9900 Stoneybrook Drive, Kensington. From Exit 33 off of I-495 west take Connecticut Avenue. At the second traffic light, turn right onto Beach Drive. Follow Beach Drive to Stoneybrook Drive and turn left. This leads to the main entrance of the visitor's center. Long before you arrive at Stoneybrook Drive, the Mormon Temple will loom before you like a fairyland castle. It is the largest structure dedicated to the Mormon Church east of the Mississippi. The temple has seven floors and is topped with six steeples. Atop one steeple is an angel weighing two and a half tons, with trumpet poised and gold leaf robes.

When the Temple was completed in 1974, it was entirely open to the public for tours. Today, while the sanctuary of the Temple is not available to the public, the visitor's center offers tours of some rooms, movies regarding the history of the Mormon Church, and a diorama of the Temple. Open daily. Free. (301) 587-0144.

SOUTHWEST AND WASHINGTON REGION

WHEATON, MD.

Wheaton is a close, convenient neighbor to Kensington, so routing to your next destination is simple. From the Mormon Temple, return to Connecticut Avenue and pick up M-193 east toward Wheaton and the Wheaton Regional Park.

WHERE TO GO

Brookside Gardens. 1500 Glenallan Avenue, Wheaton Regional Park. The 50-acre public garden is open year-round and features tropical plants, a stream, and a conservatory greenhouse. Special seasonal plantings, such as poinsettias during the Christmas holidays, are especially fine. The formal gardens are beautiful for walking and viewing. There are rose, azalea, and aquatic gardens. From early spring to the first frost, there is a wide variety of flowering plants. A special highlight is the Japanese-style garden and teahouse situated on an island with a reflecting pool. Brookside Gardens also offers lectures, courses, and workshops for the general public. Tours and special programs for adults and children are available. Open daily. Free. (301) 949-8230.

COLUMBIA, MD.

James Rouse is the dynamic developer of the "New Town" concept in America. Such instant successes as the shopping-dining formats of Faneuil Hall Market Place in Boston and Harborplace in Baltimore are but two of the tributes to his brand of genius. In 1981, more visitors strolled through Harborplace in Baltimore than Disney World in Orlando.

In the mid-60s Howard County residents saw Rouse sculpt an entirely new city out of 15,000 acres of rolling, green countryside. Columbia took shape within guidelines that ensured a harmonious interdependence of homes, businesses, churches, and commercial properties. An innovative community-based health care plan and local hospital deliver medical care with convenience and expediency. Sub-communities, or neighborhoods, are clustered around ample recreational facilities. Tasteful architecture and low-slung building complexes slip easily into the green, forested landscape.

Attractions include a shopping mall with more than 100 opportunities to "go for broke." Clothing, household items and furnishings, music stores, jewelers, and light fare dining spots are only a sample of the many shops and stops. The ubiquitous fountains and atria, which have been mimicked so frequently in other malls, add the peaceful sight and sound of flowing

SOUTHWEST AND WASHINGTON REGION

water complemented by rays of sunlight on lush plants.

In addition to the mall, there is a delightful Children's Zoo which is replete with farm animals. Nearby, the Merriweather Post Pavilion of Music is situated in a beautiful woodland setting and draws top-flight summertime entertainment ranging from the Washington National Symphony to pop performers. Enjoy reserved seats or picnic under the stars at the outer-margin grassy areas while you listen to the performances.

From Wheaton continue along M-193 east to US-29 north to Columbia. Or, if you plan to depart from Baltimore to make Columbia a single destination day trip, take US-40 west to US-29 south to Columbia.

WHERE TO GO

Columbia Exhibit Center. Little Patuxent Parkway (US-29), across from The Mall, Columbia. An audio-visual program explains the design concept of Columbia and its development plans for the future. Free exhibits depict life in the planned city. Behind the exhibit center is Lake Kittamagundi, a beautiful example of a man-made lake. Paddleboats and rowboats are available for a moderate rental fee.

The exhibit center is recommended as your first stop in Columbia to pick up a Visitor's Guide with local map and scheduled events information. Or, write ahead for this material from the Columbia Exhibit Center, Columbia, MD., 21043. Free. (301) 992-6060.

Enchanted Forest. US-40, 2.5 miles west of the junction with US-29 north. During the months of May through September, you can visit this magical attraction that is on your way back from Columbia. A 30-acre theme park based on fairytales, the Enchanted Forest delights youngsters with a variety of rides and colorful displays direct from the pages of nursery rhymes. There are animals to pet and ride, lakes, waterfalls, and a gift shop. Open May through September and weekends in October. Admission fee. Group rates available. (301) 465-0707.

From the Enchanted Forest return to Baltimore via US-40 east.

WHERE TO EAT

The Rusty Scupper. 10211 Wincopin Circle, Columbia. Here is American cuisine served abundantly and complemented by good soups and salads. Children's menu available. $$; □. (301) 992-0030.

The Mall. Little Patuxent Parkway, Columbia. Strategically located amid the 100 or so shops in The Mall are numerous eateries with varying fare. Make "mental notes" as you stroll the corridors, then select your preference. Pizza, deli, and fried chicken places compete with those featuring unusual salads and croissant combinations. Take your pick. $; usually cash only.

SOUTHWEST
And Washington Region

Day Trip 2

PRINCE GEORGE'S COUNTY: EARLY MANSIONS TOUR, MD.

Maryland has often been described as America in miniature. Our nation's history has been carved in the state's shoreline, flatlands, and mountains. Prince George's County might well be called Maryland in miniature. Similarities between the development of the county and state, and the development of the country, reveal much about our political history. These similarities are seen through historical documents and surviving public buildings. The early mansion homes, however, provide a more personal view of life in Prince George's County and America.

In these residences, an elegant domestic and social lifestyle is reflected in the beautiful settings and achievements in architecture. The dichotomy in the values of many prominent Americans is also revealed here. Early owners, for the most part, believed their wealth and high position were either the will of God or the natural order of things, despite the fact that they also believed in America's commitment to universal freedom and human dignity.

Trace the path of history and graceful living as you drive southwest. From Baltimore take the Baltimore Washington Expressway southwest (M-295) to Riverdale Road west. From Riverdale Road west, pick up the East-West Highway west (M-410) to Riverdale in Prince George's County.

The Prince George's Travel Promotion Council welcomes your requests for additional information and recommends the Early Mansions and Aerospace tours described in this day trip.

WHERE TO GO

Riversdale. (Also known as the Calvert Mansion). 4811 Riverdale Road

SOUTHWEST AND WASHINGTON REGION

in Riverdale; the mansion is located two blocks south of the East-West Highway (M-410) between US-1 and Kenilworth Avenue (M-201); it is a short distance east of the B&O Railroad tracks.

Construction of Riversdale was begun in 1801 by Baron Henri Joseph Stier, a Belgian nobleman who immigrated to America. When the Baron returned to Belgium in 1803, his daughter Rosalie and her husband George Calvert moved into the mansion and completed it. Riversdale's unique architectural design combines the functional simplicity of an American plantation home with the interior elegance of a Belgian chateau.

In 1838, Charles Benedict Calvert, the son of George and Rosalie, became proprietor of Riversdale. He was directly responsible for the founding of the Maryland Agricultural College (now the University of Maryland) and was also the prime mover behind the establishment of the U.S. Department of Agriculture. Riversdale remained in the Calvert family until 1887 and later became the home of four members of Congress. Since 1949, it has been owned and maintained by the Maryland-National Capital Park and Planning Commission.

Tours are available. Fee. (301) 779-2011. (While in the area you may want to visit the George Washington House located south of here and included in Day Trip 3 of this sector).

Montpelier. From Riversdale Mansion, return to the East-West Highway east (M-410) to Baltimore Washington Expressway north (M-295) towards Baltimore. Then take M-197 west to Muirkirk Road. Turn left onto Muirkirk Road and immediately right into the Montpelier Mansion driveway.

Montpelier, a masterpiece of Georgian architecture, was completed in the 1870s by Maj. Thomas Snowden. Throughout its long history, Montpelier has had many notable visitors. George Washington was the guest of Major Snowden twice in 1787, as he traveled to and from the Constitutional Convention in Philadelphia. In 1789, Martha Washington was the guest of the Snowdens, as she journeyed to New York for her husband's first inauguration. In 1800 Abigail Adams lodged at Montpelier on her way south to join President John Adams in the "new" White House.

In 1803 Montpelier passed to a descendant, Nicholas Snowden, who in 1824 established a successful cotton mill at the Laurel Factory (now the town of Laurel). The estate remained in the hands of the Snowden family until 1888. Later owners included diplomats and politicians. Since 1961 the property has been owned and maintained by the Maryland-National Capital Park and Planning Commission.

Tours are available. Fee. Call (301) 779-2011 for information.

Belair. 12207 Tulip Grove Drive. From Montpelier, drive east on M-197 toward Bowie for about 10 miles to Tulip Grove Drive (first intersection after junction M-197 and M-450). Turn left on Tulip Grove Drive for about ½ mile to Belair Mansion.

The central block of Belair was built in the 1740s for Provincial Gov. Samuel Ogle. It was subsequently the home of his son, Benjamin Ogle, who was an elected governor of Maryland from 1798 to 1801. There was

SOUTHWEST AND WASHINGTON REGION

considerable renovation of the interior during the residence of Benjamin Ogle, Jr., the third generation of his family to occupy Belair. It was during this time that the interior of the mansion was finished. He lived here with his large family of 14 children between 1796 and 1844.

Belair passed out of the Ogle family in 1871, and after a series of short-term owners, was purchased by James T. Woodward. In the next several years, under the care of the Woodward family, a new series of major renovations was completed, including addition of the two balancing wings. The Woodwards were famous in the thoroughbred horse racing world. The stables, which housed such famous Belair horses as Nashua, stand a short distance to the east of the mansion. The Belair mansion is currently owned by the City of Bowie.

Tours are available. No admission fee is charged, but a donation is requested. Call (301) 262-6200 for information.

Marietta. 5626 Bell Station Road. From Belair Mansion return to Tulip Grove Drive and turn right onto M-197 northwest. At M-450 west turn left for about 2¼ miles to Bell Station Road. Continue on Bell Station Road for about ¼ mile to Marietta Mansion.

Marietta was built by Judge Gabriel Duvall early in the 19th century and was his home for the last 30 years of his life. Gabriel Duvall was noted for a lifetime of public service. He served as a member of the Maryland State Legislature and the United States Congress. He was appointed Comptroller of the Treasury by President Jefferson in 1802, a position he held until his appointment to the Supreme Court by President Madison in 1811.

About the time of his appointment to the high court, Duvall began the building of Marietta, a handsome Federal-style brick house, highlighted by stone arches over each window. He added a two-story wing on the north side of the main house in the 1830s.

Duvall retired from the Supreme Court in 1835 and died at Marietta in 1844. The house remained in the possession of his descendants until 1902 and was deeded to the present owner, the Maryland-National Capital Park and Planning Commission, in 1968.

Tours are available. Fee. For information, call (301) 779-2011. From Marietta Mansion return to M-450 east to US-301 north to Baltimore.

If you have more time or would like to design a weekend package, consider taking M-450 east to a short shunt on US-301 north (Crain Highway) and pick up M-450 east again toward Annapolis, Maryland. What is generally a scenic entrance to the state's capital will turn a bit commercial as you arrive at West Street. But, drive on, as this route delivers you directly onto Church Circle in the historic district of Annapolis. From Annapolis, you might want to choose some tour options from the day trips listed in the Southeast sector. Or, continue on M-450 west to Bladensburg and Day Trip 3, this sector.

SOUTHWEST
And Washington Region

Day Trip 3

PRINCE GEORGE'S COUNTY: AEROSPACE TOUR, MD.

The entire span of American aerospace history is presented in all its richness and color in this day trip to Prince George's County. From the first balloon ascent in America, to the training of the first U.S. Army officers as airplane pilots, to the monitoring of man's journeys to the moon—it all happened here in this tour radius. The coming and going of the world's leaders at Andrews Air Force Base is witness to the continuing aerospace and aviation history-making in this area. The planning, development and monitoring of American space travel and exploration are taking place at the Goddard Space Flight Center. And, the entire history of flight is represented and preserved in the Smithsonian's Paul E. Garber Facility at Silver Hill.

Begin this day trip for an earth-bound tour of a spectrum of aviation. From Baltimore, take the Baltimore Washington Expressway southwest (M-295) to Bladensburg in Price George's County. Pick up M-450 west from M-295 to Bladensburg.

WHERE TO GO

The George Washington House. 4302 Baltimore Avenue, Bladensburg. The house stands in the median area between the north- and southbound lanes of Baltimore Avenue, just north of its intersection with M-450.

On June 17, 1784, Peter Carnes, a jack-of-all-trades, launched an unmanned hot air balloon in a field adjacent to the town of Bladensburg. This was the first documented unmanned balloon ascent in America. These early experiments were a spectacular success for both Peter Carnes and American aeronautics.

Today, five 18th-century buildings survive from the seaport town of

SOUTHWEST AND WASHINGTON REGION

Bladensburg that Carnes knew: **Bostwick,** c.1746; the **Hilleary-Magruder House,** c. 1745; **Old Clements,** c. 1760; the **Market Master's House,** c.1765, and the **George Washington House,** c. 1760; the only building of the five that is currently open for tours. It was run as a store by Carnes from 1774 to 1783. Today it serves as a museum of county history, containing dioramas depicting many important historical events and themes, including the first balloon ascent in America.

Open for tours. Fee. For information, call (301) 262-5505. While in the area, you might want to slip north to the Riversdale Mansion described in Day Trip 2 of this sector).

College Park Airport. 6709 Corporal Frank Scott Drive. Travel north on Baltimore Avenue (US-1) for about 2½ miles to Calvert Road. Turn right on Calvert Road and drive east for about ½ mile to Corporal Frank Scott Drive (immediately after the railroad track). Turn left onto Scott Drive to the College Park Airport.

College Park Airport, the "World's Oldest Continuously Operated Airport," has been associated with many of the most important people and events in aviation history. In 1909 Wilbur Wright journeyed to College Park Airport to train the first U.S. military officers to fly an airplane. In October of 1909 Lt. Frederic H. Humphreys became the first U.S. military officer to pilot an aircraft, and Mrs. Ralph Van Deman became the first woman to fly in an airplane. Later that year, Lt. George Sweet became the first Naval officer to fly in an airplane.

In the years that followed, many other dramatic aviation firsts occurred at College Park Airport, including: testing of the first bomb-dropping device (1911), the first night landing (1911), the first firing of a machine gun from an airplane in flight (1912), the first controlled helicopter flight (1924), and the first experiments with blind landing equipment and navigational aids (1927-35). In addition, the airport served as the first regularly scheduled air mail terminus in the United States (1918). College Park continues today as an operating airport and is now owned by the Maryland-National Capital Park and Planning Commission.

Free tours of the airport are available. Tours of the Airport Museum are available. Fee. For information, call (301) 779-2011.

Goddard Space Flight Center. Soil Conservation Road, Greenbelt. From College Park, travel east on Greenbelt Road (M-193) past the entrance to the Baltimore Washington Parkway and continue on to Soil Conservation Road (½ mile past the main entrance to the Goddard Space Flight Center). Turn left on Soil Conservation Road to the Visitor Center immediately on the left.

Established in 1959, Goddard Space Flight Center is one of the largest research and development facilities of the National Aeronautics and Space Administration (NASA). It is primarily responsible for the nation's near-Earth satellites; management of the design, development, and construction of spacecraft; and management of the worldwide tracking and communications network for manned and unmanned spacecraft. The center was named in honor of Robert H. Goddard, "Father of American

SOUTHWEST AND WASHINGTON REGION

Rocketry." His numerous contributions to this field provided the basis for man's entry into space exploration.

The Visitor Center at Goddard contains exhibits illustrating NASA programs: the Delta rocket mock-up on prominent display outside the museum building; Mercury, Gemini, and Apollo command modules; a moon rock sample, and an extensive satellite collection. In addition to regular museum hours, the Visitor Center hosts a model rocket launch for the public several times each month.

Adjoining the area are a convenient snack shop, picnic area, and gift shop. Parking is free. The use of cameras is encouraged.

Tours are available at no charge. For information, call (301) 344-8101.

Paul E. Garber Facility. Silver Hill Road, Silver Hill, Md. Return to M-193 and drive west (right turn) for about 2¼ miles to the Baltimore Washington Parkway (US-1). Take the Parkway south, toward Washington, then immediately south on I-95 toward Alexandria. Continue on I-95 (Captial Beltway) to Exit 11 B and drive west on M-4 for 2½ miles to Silver Hill Road (M-458). Turn left on Silver Hill Road for about 2 miles to the intersection of St. Barnabas Road (M-414), and bear right on Old Silver Hill Road. An immediate right will bring you to the parking lot of the Garber Facility.

The Garber Facility at Silver Hill, an adjunct to the National Air and Space Museum (NASM) of the Smithsonian Institution, was established in the mid-1950s as a depository for NASM's reserve collection. This "no frills" museum houses many historically significant air and space craft. It is also a storage, restoration, and preservation center. Here, the story of flight history and preservation is told in a simple, realistic setting.

Aircraft of the World War I era are on display, and a fighter plane similar to the one flown by Capt. Eddie Rickenbacker gives evidence of the courage and technical skills of early military pilots. The "Enola Gay," the B-29 that carried the first atomic bomb to Hiroshima on Aug. 6, 1945, is also housed here. In addition, the original nose cone of the Jupiter launch vehicle that carried the first monkeys into space in 1959 and set the precedents for later manned space efforts is also on display here.

Tours are available. Free. For information, call (301) 357-1400.

Andrews Air Force Base. Allentown Road. From the Garber Facility parking lot make an immediate left onto Silver Hill Road (M-458) and drive about 1 mile to Suitland Road. Turn right onto Suitland Road and drive for about 2¾ miles to Allentown Road and the main gate of Andrews Air Force Base.

The base was established in 1942 as Camp Springs Army Airfield by order of President Roosevelt. It was renamed Andrews Air Field in 1945, and in 1947 the facility was designated as Andrews Air Force Base. The base was named in honor of Lt. Gen. Frank M. Andrews who, at the time of his death in an aircraft accident in 1943, was commander of all Army Air Force operations in Europe.

Since the end of World War II, Andrews Air Force Base has served as headquarters for the Continental Air Command, Strategic Air Command,

SOUTHWEST AND WASHINGTON REGION

Military Air Transport Service, and Air Force Systems Command. During the Korean War it became a combat-readiness training base for B-25 bomber crews. During the Viet Nam War, it was the receiving station for medical evacuees, and starting in 1973 it was the homecoming station for prisoners of war.

Free tours available. Call(301) 981-4511. (From here you can go straight home by taking the Capital Beltway from Forestville Road and driving northwest back to Baltimore on M-295 north. Or, during warm weather, you might want to take advantage of the water slides and roller coasters at Wild World in Largo, Maryland.

Wild World. Largo. Take Exit 15A off the Capital Beltway (I-95) to M-214 east (Central Avenue). Take your bathing suit and challenge the water slides and Wild Wave attractions. Drier activities include roller coaster rides and other thrill-packed offerings. Fee. ☐. (301) 249-1500 or call 1-800-638-WILD, toll free.

To return to Baltimore, take Central Avenue west to the Capital Beltway and drive northwest to the Baltimore Washington Parkway (M-295N) to the city.

SOUTHWEST
And Washington Region

Day Trip 4

WASHINGTON, D.C.
GEORGETOWN, D.C.

WASHINGTON, D.C.

One sure way to "begin at the beginning" in our nation's capital is to stop at the Tourist Information Center between 14th and 15th streets on Pennsylvania Avenue N.W. in the restored Great Hall of the Department of Commerce. Located just one block from the **White House**, the center provides free maps, brochures, and touring suggestions. It is open daily from 9 A.M. to 5 P.M. or call ahead for information at (202) 789-7000. In addition, 24-hour recorded visitor information on events and happenings is available from the Washington Convention and Visitors Association's Dial-an-Event line at (202)737-8866.

From the Tourist Information Center, day trip drivers may wish to take an escorted driving tour of the city's attractions in order to get an overall perspective. Narrated shuttle tours to major sites in and around Washington offer unlimited free re-boarding, so you can visit sites at your own pace. Tickets may be purchased from the Tourmobile drivers at designated stops along the National Mall. This federal park extends from the Capitol Building grounds on the east to the Lincoln Memorial on the west between Madison and Jefferson streets. For more information regarding the Tourmobiles, call (202) 554-7950.

For general geographic orientation, here's some information that may help you to get around. **The U.S. Capitol Building,** at the east end of the Mall, is the hub of Washington's streets. The Capitol is located at the intersection of East Capitol Street, South Capitol Street, North Capitol Street, and the Mall, in lieu of a "West Capitol." The three streets and the Mall divide the city into quadrants: Northeast, Northwest, Southeast,

SOUTHWEST AND WASHINGTON REGION

and Southwest.

All numbered streets run north and south. Lettered streets run east and west. Streets with state names, such as Pennsylvania are diagonals, with the White House as the geographic center of Washington's original 10-mile square.

There are more than 100 points of interest in and around the area, along with numerous theaters and cultural opportunities. It is best to write in advance and get information you'll need to make your day trip more enjoyable. Your requests are welcome at the Washington, D.C., Convention and Visitors Association, 1575 Eye Street, N.W., Washington, D.C. 20005. (202) 789-7000. In the meantime here are a few of the delights to be sampled in the area.

WHERE TO GO

U.S. Capitol Building. Intersection of East Capitol Street, South Capitol Street, North Capitol Street, and the Mall. Explore the cradle of our country's politics. Its famous 180-foot white dome presides over the Rotunda and the adjoining House of Representatives and the Senate. Visitors are invited to view debates on the floor of the House or Senate. Passes to the galleries may be obtained for U.S. citizens from their state senators or representatives.

Foreign visitors should apply to the office of the Sergeant at Arms of the Senate. Free tours of the Rotunda, Statuary Hall (with two statues from each state), the House of Representatives (the largest legislative chamber in the world), the Senate (with its famous reception room), and the Crypt (the original site of the Supreme Court) are designed for about 30 to 40 minutes of touring time. Open daily for tours except Thanksgiving, Christmas, and New Year's Day.

Washington Monument. East end of the National Mall at 15th Street. Dedicated in 1885 to the memory of our first U.S. president, this 555-foot obelisk is the world's largest masonry structure. Adventurous visitors may enjoy the panoramic view from atop its observation area. Open daily. Fee.

Lincoln Memorial. West Potomac Park and 23rd Street N.W. Looking west across 17th Street, the peaceful beauty of the Reflecting Pool gives way to the Grecian-like temple that is a monument to our 16th president. The 19-foot statue of Abraham Lincoln is as inspiring to visitors as the words from his speeches that are carved in the surrounding walls. The western view from the Memorial encompasses the Potomac River and the Arlington National Cemetery on its western bank.

The Ellipse. Looking north from the Washington monument at the National Mall, just beyond Constitution Avenue. This comely, flowered park is a favorite spot of quiet and solitude for nearby office workers and visitors. At the northern edge is Pennsylvania Avenue N.W. and the White House.

The White House. 1600 Pennsylvania Avenue, N.W. This has been the home of every U.S. president since 1800. Five rooms of the 132-room mansion are open for tours. Open daily, Tuesday through Saturday. Closed

Christmas, New Year's Day, and during presidential functions. Free. (202)456-7041.

The National Gallery of Art. Fourth Street and Constitution Avenue N.W. The gallery features extensive collections of Western European and American works. (202) 737-4215.

The Smithsonian Institution Museum Group. On the Mall between Constitution Avenue to the north and Independence Avenue to the south. Included within these walls are many important collections. **The Museum of Natural History,** 10th and Constitution Avenue N.W., contains collections of fellow earth inhabitants ranging from the far corners of the globe and prehistoric eras.

The National Air and Space Museum, 6th Street and Independence Avenue N.W., features the history of aviation from the original aircraft of the Wright Brothers to present-day, state-of-the-art satellites and rockets.

The Hirshhorn Museum and Sculpture Garden, 8th Street and Independence Avenue N.W., displays an astounding collection of 19th-and 20th-century art, including works of Matisse, Picasso, and Rodin.

General visitor information regarding the Smithsonian Group may be obtained by calling (202) 357-2700. 9 A.M. to 5 P.M. daily. Recorded event information is available at (202) 357-2020.

GEORGETOWN, D.C.

While in Washington, be sure to visit Georgetown which is located mainly along M Street and Wisconsin Avenue in the southwest sector of the city. Numerous small shops feature excellent values in glassware, wood, fabrics, clothing, and books.

More opportunities abound in **Georgetown Park,** a new Victorian-style edifice which occupies a square block between M Street and the C&O Canal. Within the elaborately decorated, three-tiered building are a variety of restaurants and specialty shops ranging from reasonable to expensive.

Georgetown's **M Street** features some of the best entertainment in Washington. Excellent jazz and live stand-up comedy are profiled against the pomp and grandeur of the nation's capital. Dining spots are plentiful. From the creative concoctions of the natural food store, to the hearty fare of the popular pubs, to the elegant offerings of the Georgetown Inn, it's all here for your pleasure.

Many of the other destinations listed in the day trips of the Southwest sector would make excellent adjuncts to this tour if you want to design an itinerary beyond the two-hour guidelines.

From Washington, select New York Avenue northbound to leave the city. This road becomes the Baltimore Washington Parkway (M-295) and will easily lead you back to Baltimore.

SOUTHWEST
And Washington Region

Day Trip 5

ARLINGTON, VA.
ALEXANDRIA, VA.
MOUNT VA.
Worth More Time:
MANASSAS, VA.

ARLINGTON, VA.

Situated on the south bank of the Potomac River is the second smallest county in the United States. Arlington, a suburb of Washington, D.C., was developed over approximately 25 square miles of the northern tip of Virginia. From Baltimore take US-40 west to US-29 south to Washington. In Washington continue south on US-29, which is New Hampshire Avenue. Follow it around Washington Circle to pick up US-240 southeast (23rd Street) to the Lincoln Memorial. From the Lincoln Memorial pick up the Arlington Memorial Bridge into the Arlington National Cemetery.

WHERE TO GO

Arlington National Cemetery. Located on the Virginia side of the Arlington Memorial Bridge. Established in 1864, Arlington is the best known of all the national cemeteries. The ownership of the original parcel of land upon which the cemetery was developed is traced back to George Washington. Through a network of marriages and inheritances, it became the property of Robert E. Lee.

For many people, a visit to this national landmark is an opportunity to pay personal respects to the soldiers of the Tomb of the Unknowns and the graves of President John F. Kennedy and Senator Robert F. Kennedy.

President Kennedy's grave is marked by an eternal flame and quotations from his inaugural address. Nearby are the graves of his two infant children. The Tomb of the Unknowns is guarded 24 hours a day by the "Old Guard" 3rd U.S. Infantry Regiment. A precision ceremony of the changing of the guard takes place every half-hour in the daytime from April through the end of September, every hour for the remainder of the year, and every two hours at night.

Buried in the National Cemetery are George Washington, Parke Custis and Mrs. Custis, Pierre L'Enfant, William Howard Taft, Gen. John J. Pershing, Robert E. Peary, Rear Adm. Richard E. Byrd, John Foster Dulles, and many other famous Americans.

The cemetery is open daily, year-round. Parking is at the visitor's center on Eisenhower Drive where special passes are distributed to family members and friends of those buried here. Otherwise, for the general public, Tourmobiles leave the visitor's center for regularly scheduled narrated tours of the major points of interest. Fee. (202) 554-7950.

Arlington House. Just above the cemetery as you enter from the Arlington Memorial Bridge sits the house of Robert E. Lee and his bride, Mary Anna Randolph Custis. The building was begun in 1802 by George Washington Parke Custis, grandson of Martha Washington. The Lees occupied the house from 1831 to 1861. It was here, in 1861, that Lee made his fateful decision to resign his commission in the U.S. Army in order to defend his native state. When Lee was attending to the Confederate troops in Richmond, Union forces occupied the house, because of its position, which commanded approaches to Washington. They buried their dead on the slopes beneath it.

The property was confiscated by the government in 1864 due to non-payment of taxes. A Lee descendant sued for the return of the property in 1864 and won. By then, however, thousands of graves covered the estate and the property was sold back to the government for $150,000. Now administered by the National Park Service, the mansion is being restored to its 1861 appearance along with the return of some of the original furnishings of the Custis and Lee families. Open for tours. Free. (703) 557-0613.

ALEXANDRIA, VA.

Alexandria, a seaport town with a rich maritime and trading heritage, is located on the Potomac River across from Washington, D.C. It was founded by Scottish merchants in 1749, and clipper ships brought a booming tobacco trade here to the Potomac River shores. George Washington came on horseback to worship in the city and meet with fellow patriots as the nation's first fight for freedom began.

Today, Alexandria boasts 106,000 residents and visitors from around

SOUTHWEST AND WASHINGTON REGION

the world. Tradition lives in the historic homes, churches, and taverns beautifully preserved like a colonial sampler. The rich heritage and colorful past live also in the many specialty shops and art galleries housed in restored 18th- and 19th-century buildings.

In this veritable melting pot of nationalities, excellent restaurants feature French, Greek, Afghan, Scottish, Italian, Creole, and (Ah, yes!) traditional American colonial fare.

Alexandria could be a single-destination day trip if you prefer. It lends itself beautifully to a walking tour, which is described below. Many historic sites are within a stroll of one another. Shopping is particularly interesting and colorful, and the day trip visitor can top off the tour with a variety of choices for dining. To see the town at its best, consult the Alexandria Tourist Council, which recommends a walking tour of the sites listed below.

From Baltimore take the Baltimore Washington Expressway (M-295) toward Washington. Then, pick up the Capital Beltway southeast (I-95, alternately designated I-495) and drive to US-1 north into Alexandria. Enter Alexandria on Patrick Street (US-1 N) and drive to King Street (V-7). Or, if you plan to travel from Arlington, take Henry G. Shirley Memorial Highway south to Alexandria.

WHERE TO GO

The Ramsay House. 221 King Street. Your first stop on a tour of Alexandria should be the Ramsay House. Now the official visitor's center, it is a reconstruction of the original house which was built c. 1724 and moved by barge up-river to its present resting site after Alexandria was established in 1749. William Ramsay, Alexandria's first postmaster, was a Scottish merchant and city founder. The offices of the Alexandria Tourist Council are also located here. Open daily. Free. (703) 549-0205.

The Stabler-Leadbeater Apothecary Shop. 107 S. Fairfax Street. The Apothecary Shop was founded in 1792 and was in continuous operation until 1933. The building displays a remarkable collection of early medical ware and handblown glass containers. The original furnishings and glassware have never been removed. Open for tours. Donations accepted. (703) 836-3713.

The Old Presbyterian Meeting House. 321 Fairfax Street. Built in 1774 by Scottish founders of Alexandria, the Meeting House served as a gathering place for patriots.

George Washington's funeral sermons were preached here in 1799 when bad weather made roads to Christ Church impassable. The graveyard is the site of the Tomb of the Unknown Soldier of the American Revolution and of grave markers for Col. Dennis Ramsay and other esteemed Alexandrians. Open for tours. Free. (703) 549-6670.

The Athenaeum. 201 Prince Street. The building is one of Alexandria's significant examples of Greek Revival architecture and was built as a banking house about 1850. It now is the gallery of the Northern Virginia Fine Arts Association, an affiliate of the Virginia Museum of Fine Arts. Open for tours. Free; donations accepted. Closed during the summer months. (703) 548-0035.

The Torpedo Factory Art Center. 105 N. Union Street. The Art Center houses the studios of nearly 200 professional artists and craftsmen who create and sell on the premises. Originally a torpedo shell case factory built in 1918, the Art Center is an imaginative example of adaptive re-use. Open daily. Free. (703) 838-4565.

The Alexandria Archeology. 105 N. Union Street. This program is one of the few such American research facilities devoted to the conservation of sites in an urban development. The city-operated laboratory and exhibit area are located in the Torpedo Factory. Free. (703) 838-4399.

The Carlyle House. 121 N. Fairfax Street. Alexandria's "grandest" home was built in 1752 by the Scottish merchant John Carlyle. Design of the Carlyle House was thought to be inspired by Craigiehall, an imposing stone manor house in Scotland. In the spring of 1755, Gen. Edward Braddock made Carlyle House his Alexandria headquarters. At a meeting in the home's elegant great parlor, Braddock and five colonial governors planned the strategy and funding of the early campaigns of the French and Indian War. Open for tours. Fee. (703) 549-2997.

Market Square. 300 block of King Street. In 1749, two half-acre lots were set aside during the survey of the city for a market place and town hall which was constructed in 1752. Over the years schools, jails, whipping posts, private fire companies, and, in 1817, a bell and clock tower were added. After a fire in 1871, a U-shaped Victorian building with its front on Cameron Street and two wings along Fairfax and Royal Streets were built with a central courtyard which housed the market. An addition in 1962 has closed the "U", but the market, the oldest continuously-operating market in the country, is still held early on Saturday mornings. (703) 838-4000.

Gadsby's Tavern Museum. 134 N. Royal Street. Known for its outstanding Georgian architecture, Gadsby's Tavern Museum consists of two important buildings built around 1770 and 1792. The tavern was a center of political, business, and social life in early Alexandria. Celebrations honoring George Washington were held in the second floor ballroom to music played from a hanging gallery. Open for tours. Fee. (703) 838-4242.

Boyhood Home of Robert E. Lee. 607 Oronoco Street. "Light Horse Harry" Lee, Revolutionary War hero and father of Robert E. Lee, brought his family to this house in 1812. Lee lived and studied here in his early childhood years. The preserved house is beautifully furnished with rare antiques and Lee memorabilia. Open for tours. Fee. (703) 548-8454.

Lee-Fendall House. 614 Oronoco Street. A long line of Lees lived in and visited this rambling wooden structure built in 1789 by Philip Fendall. He was a member of a prominent Charles County, Maryland, family and had three wives, all Lee women. In this house "Light Horse Harry" wrote the farewell address from the citizens of Alexandria when Washington left Mount Vernon to become the first president of the United States. Open for tours. Fee. (703) 548-1789.

The Lloyd House. 220 N. Washington Street. One of Alexandria's

SOUTHWEST AND WASHINGTON REGION

finest examples of late-Georgian architecture, the Lloyd House was built in 1797. Known for its association with the Lee family, the house was purchased in 1832 by John Lloyd whose wife Anne Harriotte Lee was a cousin of Robert E. Lee. It was owned by the Lloyd family until 1918. Restored for adaptive use in 1976, the building is now part of the Alexandria Library and houses an extensive collection of rare books, records, and documents on city and Virginia history. Open to the public. Free. (703) 838-4577.

Christ Church. Cameron and North Washington streets. This English country-style church was built between 1767 and 1773 of native brick and stone. George Washington was on the vestry; the church contains his family pew. Robert E. Lee was confirmed here and later attended from Arlington House. Open to the public. Donations accepted. (703) 549-1450.

The Lyceum. 201 S. Washington Street. This example of Greek Revival architecture was built in 1839 as a cultural center for Alexandria. In 1974 it was restored and became the nation's first Bicentennial Center. Today it is a museum and center for the comprehensive history of Alexandria. The Office of Historic Alexandria is also located here. Open daily. Free. Educational tours arranged. Gift shop on the premises. (703) 838-4994.

The George Washington Masonic National Memorial. King Street and Callahan Drive. The memorial contains outstanding Washington memorabilia, including the family Bible and a clock that was stopped at the time of his death. Large murals and stained-glass windows depict events of Washington's life. Open daily. Free. (707) 683-2007.

Fort Ward Museum and Historic Site. 4301 W. Braddock Road. Owned and operated by the City of Alexandria, Fort Ward is the only Union fort in the defenses of Washington developed as a major Civil War site. The re-constructed museum contains one of the finest collections of Civil War objects. The 40-acre park includes a restored bastion, outdoor amphitheater, and picnic facilities. Free. (703) 838-4848.

MOUNT VERNON

Travel south along the scenic Potomac River toward the historic beauty of Mount Vernon. No wonder George Washington selected this territory for his estate. "No estate in United America is more pleasantly situated," commented General Washington. The broad sweep of the Potomac, pastoral fields, and beautifully forested areas easily lend themselves to the traditional colonial Virginia lifestyle. From Alexandria follow the Mount Vernon Memorial Highway south (V-233) (also designated the George Washington Parkway) along the shores of the Potomac River to Mount Vernon.

SOUTHWEST AND WASHINGTON REGION

WHERE TO GO

Mount Vernon. Follow V-233 south to its terminus at V-235 west and north, 8 miles south of Alexandria. The exhibition area contains more than 30 acres with several miles of walks and lanes for the visitor to explore. The Mansion is, of course, the focal point of any visit to Mount Vernon. Designed and enlarged from the one-and-one-half-story farmhouse of his youth by George Washington, the Mansion is a unique and beautiful example of mid-Georgian architecture. Fourteen rooms are shown, which exhibit numerous original furnishings that have been returned through gift, loan, and purchase since 1858. In that year, the nucleus of the estate was purchased from Washington heirs by the Mount Vernon Ladies' Association in a pioneering example of historic preservation.

Close to the Mansion are the north and south service lanes where small, white wooden buildings accommodated the domestic servants and cottage industries which helped sustain the economy of this successful plantation. Nine outbuildings are furnished and open, in addition to the Museum on the North Lane with its large collection of silver, porcelain, military equipment, and other collections. In the nearby brick greenhouse and slave quarters building is a small museum which helps explain the architectural development and restoration of the Mansion.

The colonnades lead from the Mansion on the west to the kitchen and former Servants Hall. The two-story piazza on the east allows a view of the mile-wide Potomac River. The rural character of the Maryland shore beyond is now preserved as a National Park, ensuring that the majestic view so enjoyed by the Washingtons and visitors for two centuries will remain unchanged for future generations to enjoy. Open daily. Fee. (703) 780-2000.

Woodlawn Plantation. From Mount continue west on V-235 to US-1 and the site of Woodlawn Plantation. The rich heritage of northern Virginia is epitomized by this property, once part of George Washington's Dogue Run Farm. The retired president gave the estate to his adopted daughter, Eleanor Parke Custis, and his nephew Lawrence Lewis as a wedding gift. The couple then commissioned Dr. William Thornton, architect of the U.S. Capitol, to design the Georgian mansion. Today it is a property of the National Trust for Historic Preservation, and thousands of visitors enjoy the stately restored mansion with its Federal-style rooms and its broad vista of the Potomac River. Open daily for tours with the exception of Christmas, New Year's Day, and Thanksgiving. Fee. (703) 557-7881.

Continue on US-1 south past **Pohick Church** at Telegraph and Old Colchester roads. This landmark along the way to Gunston Hall is an Anglican church designed in 1774 by James Wren under the advisement of George Washington. It is open to the public and listed on the National Register of Historic Sites. At V-242 east turn left and arrive at Gunston Hall.

SOUTHWEST AND WASHINGTON REGION

Gunston Hall. George Mason, Father of the Bill of Rights, created this magnificent Georgian home overlooking the Potomac River near Mount Vernon. Mason's colonial plantation home was complete with outbuildings, extensive formal gardens, and even a deer park. It was a self-sufficient plantation and consisted of more than 5,000 acres devoted to growing wheat and tobacco and grazing sheep. Tiny village-like compounds on the grounds provided housing for craftsmen, servants, and slaves who lived there with their families.

The house was designed and begun before 1755, and Mason called upon the renowned William Buckland to give it the finishing architectural touches and to design the superb carvings as Buckland would later do in many other fine homes of Virginia and Maryland.

From Gunston Hall, return on V-242 west to US-1 north toward Alexandria for an alternate route. Then pick up I-495 east around Washington on the Capital Beltway to the Baltimore Washington Parkway north (M-295) for return routing to Baltimore, or continue on to Manassas, if time permits.

WORTH MORE TIME

Although it is more than two hours from Baltimore, **Manassas, Virginia,** is a "must do" for American history and Civil War buffs. Manassas set the stage for the first major encounter in the war between the states. Houses and architecture reflect the Victorian design which was the style when the town was chartered in 1873. Walking tour recommendations may be obtained at the Greater Manassas Chamber of Commerce located at 1900 Center Street near Main. Or call ahead for information at (703) 368-4813. From Gunston Hall continue on US-1 south to Dumfries, Virginia. Then pick up V-234 west (Dumfries Road) into Manassas.

WHERE TO GO

Manassas Museum. 9406 Main Street. This two-story building served as the first bank of Manassas. Civil War artifacts, local memorabilia, and rotating collections are among the exhibitions. Free. (703) 368-1873.

Manassas National Battlefield. The Park Visitor Center is located on V-234 between I-66 and US-29. Two great battles of the Civil War—the First and Second Battles of Manassas, also known as the battles of Bull Run—were fought here. It was on this battlefield that Gen. Thomas J. Jackson earned the nickname of Stonewall Jackson for standing firm against the Union forces.

The visitor center contains a museum, a slide program, and a battle map. Open daily. Closed Christmas Day. Free. For more information, call the Greater Manassas Chamber of Commerce at (703) 368-4813.

Return routing is begun on V-234 east toward Dumfries. Then pick up

SOUTHWEST AND WASHINGTON REGION

US-1 north toward Alexandria and follow the recommended directions to Baltimore listed at the conclusion of Gunston Hall in this section.

WHERE TO STAY

Econo Lodge. 7249 New Market Court. Located on V-234 just south of the Manassas exit of I-66. Open all year. $$; ☐. (703) 369-1700.

Ramada Inn. 7104 Sudley Road. Located just south of the Manassas exit of I-66 on V-234. Restaurant on the premises. Open all year. $$; ☐. (703) 783-3193.

WHERE TO EAT

Brady's Public House. 9412 Main Street, Manassas. Relaxing Irish-American atmosphere. Light fare, soup, and sandwiches for lunch. $-$$; ☐. (703) 369-1469.

St. James Place. 9112-B Center Street. Live lobster, steak Diane, and veal Oscar are some of the house specialties here. $-$$; ☐. (703) 368-6230.

SOUTHWEST
And Washington Region

Day Trip 6

GREAT FALLS OF THE POTOMAC, MD.
C&O CANAL NATIONAL HISTORICAL PARK, MD.

GREAT FALLS OF THE POTOMAC, MD.

About 15 miles northwest of Washington, D.C., is a series of picturesque falls and rapids. Here the Potomac River roars through a rocky cataract, dropping more than 50 feet to a narrow gorge.

From Baltimore take the Baltimore Washington Expressway south (M-295) to the Capital Beltway west (I-495) to Exit 41 at MacArthur Boulevard. While this may seem to be a fast-track start to an otherwise peaceful day, this routing avoids some of the snarls of the Washington suburb areas. Take MacArthur Boulevard west to Great Falls.

WHERE TO GO

C&O Canal Museum. 11710 MacArthur Boulevard. Built in 1828 as an inn and lockhouse, Crommelin House (Great Falls Tavern) soon developed a reputation for hospitality along the great canal. Today that tradition lives at the visitor's center and museum located here. The museum features a scale model of a barge going through a lock and the canal. Other exhibits include a history of the canal. Two films, "Down the Old Potomac" and "The C&O Canal," are shown continuously. Open year-round. Closed holidays. Free. (301) 299-3613.

C&O Barge Trips. Available from the visitor's center located at the Great Falls Tavern, these one-and-a-half-hour tours of the canal are conducted aboard a mule drawn, 19th-century-style barge. This living history lesson is given by costumed guides and includes performances of typical tasks of the era and a presentation of period music. Trips also originate in Georgetown at the landing between Thomas Jefferson and 30th streets. Fee. For information on schedules and charges, phone (301) 299-2026.

C&O CANAL NATIONAL HISTORICAL PARK, MD.

Pack your picnic cooler and wear your hiking shoes and comfortable clothing for this day trip to the C&O Canal. Get ready for a nature-loving departure from sophisticated shopping and stately mansions. Enjoy your favorite form of getting next to nature: walking, biking, hiking, or camping.

Beginning at the Maryland side of the Potomac River in Georgetown, the canal extends for 184.5 miles to Cumberland, Maryland. Along the way it passes many sites of natural beauty and historical value. Locks and lockhouses, dams, aqueducts, mule barns, and remnants of once-thriving communities remind us of almost a century of active canal traffic. The canal was begun in 1828 with a dedication by President John Quincy Adams and was proclaimed a National Monument in 1960 by President Dwight Eisenhower.

To compensate for the difference in elevation from Washington to Cumberland and to ensure smooth waters in the canal, 74 lift locks were built. Initially each lock was known by a number, but as individual locktenders became well known, their names were used for identification, as in Swains Lock and Pennyfield Lock.

Because locking barge traffic through was a day and night operation, lockhouses were built by the canal company to house the lock tenders and their families. It was also necessary to build aqueducts to carry the canal across the numerous tributaries that flow into the Potomac River. These impressive structures were major engineering accomplishments in their time.

From the visitor's center at Great Falls Tavern on the C&O Canal, drive east on MacArthur Boulevard to Falls Road and turn right. Drive northeast on Falls Road to M-190 and turn left. Continue west on M-190 to points of interest in the park.

WHERE TO GO

Swains Lock. Also designated lock #21, this lock is just west of the Great Falls Tavern on M-190. Picnic facilities, drinking water, and overnight camping are available. For specific information call the Great Falls Tavern. (301) 299-3613.

Pennyfield Lock. Also designated lock #22, it is located 3 miles west

SOUTHWEST AND WASHINGTON REGION

on M-190 from Swains Lock. Here are particularly nice picnic facilities for the day trip visitor. Plan to have your picnic lunch here or continue to Seneca.

Seneca. A bit farther west on M-190, just past lock # 23 (Violets Lock), is Seneca, which offers picnic facilities and a boat ramp. For specific boating information, call the Great Falls Tavern. (301) 299-3613.

The C&O Canal route offers many such stops with conveniences ranging from picnic facilities to drive-in and group camping areas. Information centers and campfire programs are also offered. For points west of Seneca and for general park information, call (301) 739-4200 or write the Park Superintendent, C&O Canal National Historical Park, Box 4, Sharpsburg, Maryland, 21782.

WHAT TO DO

Canoeing. Canoeing on short and widely separated stretches of the canal is a popular recreation in the park. Maps which would be helpful to the visitor can be obtained by writing the U.S. Geological Survey, Branch of Distribution, 1200 Eads Street, Arlington, Virginia, 22202, or by phoning (703) 557-2751. The U.S. Weather Bureau provides a telephone message for those interested in river conditions in the lower Potomac Valley. (202) 899-3210.

Cycling. Many cyclists enjoy the towpath on the canal. Ambitious travelers tackle the entire 184.5 miles between Cumberland and Georgetown. Others are content with shorter outings. Three sections lend themselves to one-day bike trips. The towpath in these areas is in good condition and the scenery is great! These areas include: Great Falls Tavern to Georgetown, 14 miles; Fifteen Mile Creek to Paw Paw Tunnel, 15 miles; and Dam 4 to Lock # 33, 24 miles. There is access by motor vehicle to either end of these areas.

Be sure to contact the park superintendent as previously listed for general maps and timely detour information. (301) 739-4200.

Fishing. Fishing has long been one of the most popular activities for visitors to the park. The Potomac contains a number of game species, including bass, catfish, carp, sunfish, and shad. Areas recommended for fishing are North Branch, Oldtown, Seneca, Big Pool, and Little Pool. For specific information regarding regulations and other details, obtain the latest Maryland Sportfishing Guide by contacting the Information Division, Department of Natural Resources, Tawes State Office Building, Annapolis, Maryland, 21401. Park rangers on patrol are also knowledgeable resources for this information.

Camping. All campsites are on a first-come, first-served basis except Marsden Tract, which must be reserved ahead. (301) 299-3613.

Stay is limited to 14 days at the drive-in areas, 10 days at the "carry-in" and 1 night at each hiker-biker area per trip. Conveniences, facilities, and regulations will vary with each site, so write or phone ahead to the park superintendent, as previously described, for details.

Return to Baltimore via M-190 east to the Capital Beltway east (I-495).

SOUTHWEST AND WASHINGTON REGION

Then pick up the Baltimore Washington Parkway north (M-295) to Baltimore.

If you're planning an overnight trip, you may want to select some of the destinations described in the day trips of the Western sector in the following chapter. The carefully selected secondary roads described in that sector's day trips will take you on a scenic route to Harpers Ferry, Virginia, and Antietam, Maryland, among other such attractions.

SOUTHWEST
And Washington Region

Day Trip 7

MIDDLEBURG, VA.
LEESBURG, VA.
WATERFORD, VA.
POINT OF ROCKS, MD.

MIDDLEBURG, VA.

The unofficial capital of the "Hunt Country" of Virginia, Middleburg was first known as an overnight stagecoach stop with its convenient location midway between Alexandria and Winchester. Today, many visitors are attracted to this picturesque little community and the many Hunt Country events. Such activities as the Glenwood Steeplechase and Carriage Drive in the spring, the Loudon Junior and Pony Show in June, and the Middleburg Wine Festival in autumn proudly show off the best of this beautiful wine and horse country. Unique shops and delightful restaurants make Middleburg an enjoyable place to visit.

From Baltimore take the Baltimore Washington Expressway south (M-295) to the Capital Beltway west (I-495) to US-50 west into Middleburg.

Meredyth Vineyards. From US-50 at Middleburg take V-776 south for 2½ miles to V-628. Turn right and drive west for 2½ miles to the entrance of Meredyth Vineyards. This is one of Virginia's largest commercial vineyards, with 55 acres of French-American and European (vinifera) vines. Wines include Aurora Blanc, de Chaunac, Seyval Blanc, Chardonnay, Riesling, Cabernet Sauvignon, Villard Blanc, and Villard Noir. Visitors are invited to tour the vineyards and see French-American vines from nursery to bearing vineyard rows, as well as Asiatic-European vinifera. Guides are most helpful in explaining the vineyard's methods and answering your questions. Tours are daily without need for appointments. Groups greater than 10 people should arrange for tours in advance, and a nominal group rate is charged. (703) 687-6277.

Piedmont Vineyards and Winery, Inc. From U.S.-50 at Middleburg take V-626 south for approximately 3 miles to the Piedmont Vineyards. Piedmont seems to be as proud of its 30 acres of fine vineyards as it is proud of its knowledgeable founder, Mrs. Thomas Furness. Beginning with vineyard plantings in 1973, Mrs. Furness aspired to produce the finest quality white wines. She is the only woman to date who has single-handedly started a vineyard and winery operation. Mrs. Furness was 75 at the time of Piedmont's inception. Acres of Chardonnay, Semillon, and Seyval Blanc are thriving with modern techniques and old-world formulas. Tours are given without charge. Fee charged for groups greater than 10 people. (703)687-5134.

LEESBURG, VA.

Originally called Georgetown in honor of King George II, Leesburg was chartered by the English Crown in 1757 to have 70 half-acre lots and six streets. Shortly thereafter a bill was introduced to rename Georgetown Leesburgh (now Leesburg), in honor of Thomas Lee. Located between the Potomac River and Blue Ridge Mountains in the rolling countryside of northern Virginia, Leesburg takes you through two centuries of American history with authentic buildings of diverse architecture. Narrow streets, brick sidewalks, quaint shops, and a variety of fine restaurants add up to a fun day trip experience. Designated an Historic District by the Virginia Landmarks Commission, Leesburg has especially worth while walking tours. Bring your camera or your sketch pad to "capture" the architecture of original, historic buildings and scenes of easy, Southern life.

WHERE TO GO

Loudoun Museum and Information Center. 16 W. Loudoun Street, Leesburg, VA, 22075. A free, beautifully illustrated map of a self-guided walking tour of the town is available from the Information Center. The address is included here in the event that you might want to write ahead for this handy guide. Also available at the Information Center are a wide variety of local artifacts on exhibit and an orientation slide presentation. Free. Next door, in a restored 18th-century log cabin, local craftsmen in period costume demonstrate skills such as pottery making, weaving, spinning, quilting, and fine art demonstrations. Free. (703) 777-0519 or 471-6093.

Oatlands. Located approximately 6 miles south of Leesburg on US-15. You may want to tour this beautiful Classical Revival mansion and plantation first, while en route to Leesburg from Middleburg.

Located in the heart of northern Virginia's hunt country, this marvelous mansion was once the center of a thriving 3,400-acre plantation. Oatlands House, constructed shortly after 1800, was partially remodeled in 1827. A front portico with hand-carved Corinthian capitals was added later. Confederate troops were billeted in the house during the Civil War. Boxwood, magnolias, and a gazebo grace the terraced formal gardens planned by Oatland's builder, George Carter, a great-grandson of famed planter Robert "King" Carter. Greek Revival ornament adorns an interior filled with French and American art and antiques.

Springtime visitors to the property enjoy the Loudoun Hunt Point-to-Point races in mid-April and a foxhound show in May. Today, the beauty of Oatlands and its 261 acres of farmland is protected by a series of scenic easements, which insure the estate's continuing role as a center of cultural life and equestrian sports in Loudoun County, Virginia. Oatlands is a property of the National Trust for Historic Preservation. Open for tours daily from April to mid-November. Fee. (703) 777-3174.

Morven Park. Located at the western end of Leesburg. Take US-7 west to Old Waterford Road and the entrance of Morven Park. Enter the 1,200 acres of this Virginia estate down a tree-lined, mile-long drive past formal boxwood gardens to the stately mansion. The mansion, focal point of the estate, evolved from a fieldstone farmhouse in 1781 to its present turn-of-the-century appearance. Enter the mansion through a Greek Revival portico to see a Renaissance great hall, a Jacobean dining room, a French drawing room, and library. Furnishings include 16th-century Flemish tapestries, fine paintings, and porcelain figurines.

In addition to the magnificent mansion, extensive formal gardens, and nature trails, there is a carriage museum—housing more than 100 horse-drawn vehicles. Throughout the year, equestrian events are held on the grounds. Open weekends, May through October 17th, and daily from Memorial Day through Labor Day. Fee. (703) 777-2414.

WHERE TO EAT

Sigwick Inn and Golf Club. US-15 south at the US-7 by-pass in Leesburg. Excellent food, service, and atmosphere at reasonable prices. Candlelit dining room furnished with old country antiques. There's a scenic view from the terrace. Outstanding Friday night seafood buffet and Sunday brunch and buffet. Motel adjoining. $$; □. (703) 777-1910 or toll free 1-800-ABC-ROOM.

WATERFORD, VA.

Two and one half centuries of history are preserved in this tiny village clustered around a mill on the banks of the Catoctin Creek. Settled in

1733 by Quakers from Pennsylvania, the village hasn't grown since the mid-19th century. Today the brick, stone, and frame buildings are still nestled quietly in the Catoctin Valley, surrounded by the fertile, rolling farmland of northwestern Virginia. In 1970 the entire village—houses, barns, shops, schools, churches, and fields—was designated a National Historic Landmark. Waterford is not a restoration, but a living village, where the past mingles with the present in an unbroken line of events. From Leesburg take V-7 west to V-662 north to Waterford.

With the exception of a three-day Homes Tour and Crafts Exhibit which is held each year in early October (most properties are privately owned and occupied), village residences are not open for tours. Visits to Waterford are best planned from the perspective of a self-guided walking tour through its charming streets. While the commercialism of restaurants has not come to the area, local residents feel that the best place to start your visit here is at the friendly Waterford Market on Factory Street. Here, a country store environment offers light refreshment at a modest price and well-seasoned tourist advice for free. Open Monday through Saturday.

POINT OF ROCKS, MD.

Point of Rocks was a strategic site during the Civil War. While no major encounters took place here, there were many skirmishes and raids. It was here that Gen. Joseph Hooker received telegraphed orders to turn over the Army of the Potomac to General Meade just before the Battle of Gettysburg.

The area received national attention in 1830 when the proponents of the B&O Railroad and the C&O Canal fought over the right of way on the narrow strip of land here between the base of Catoctin Mountain and the Potomac.

Today visitors enjoy the prime fishing waters here. Day trip drivers will find it to be a scenic drive at the end of this busy itinerary.

From Waterford take V-662 south to V-7 east to Leesburg, then go north on US-15 to Point of Rocks. For return routing to Baltimore at the end of this day trip, continue east on M-28 to M-85 north and pick up I-70 east (just outside of Frederick) to Baltimore.

Covered bridge, Thurmont, Maryland

WEST

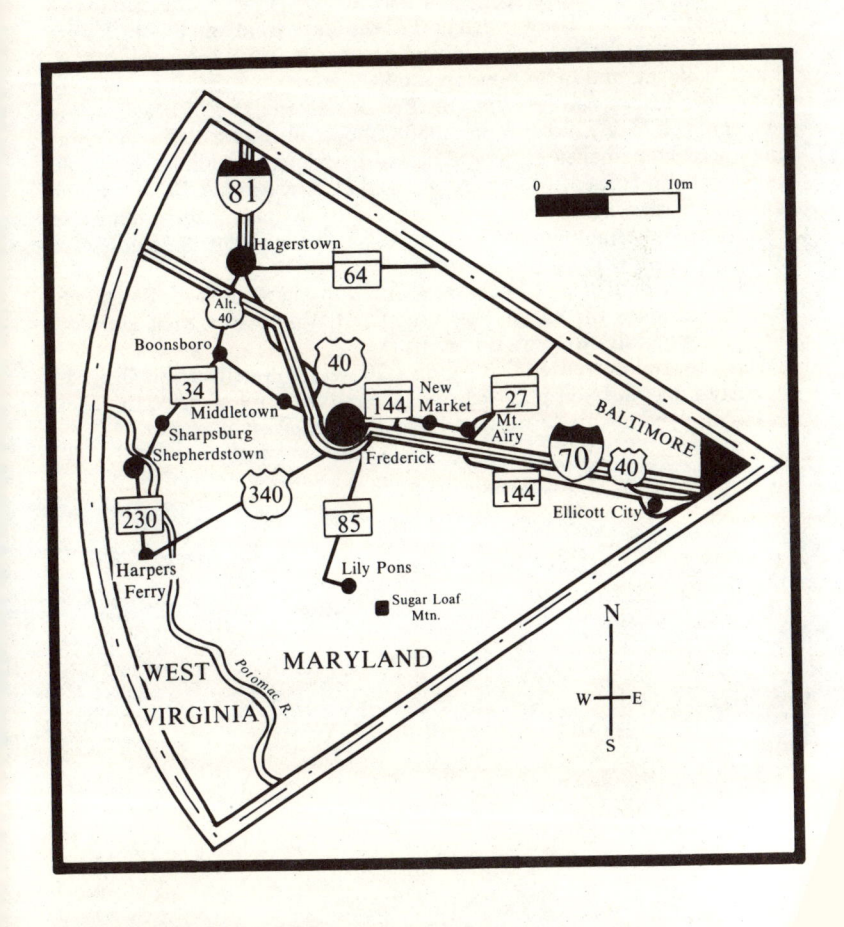

WEST

Travel west to a route rich in cultural history. This fertile approach to the Piedmont region attracted a diverse mixture of peoples—English, Scotch, and German. Rich farmland and prolific fur trapping brought increasing numbers of settlements as the population eased itself westward toward new markets. This corridor became a mecca for ambitious young Americans approaching the gateway to the western frontier. Vital north-south and east-west trade routes were established as towns prospered.

Towns grew around grist, paper, and saw mills, which functioned as centers for trade. In the western part of the state grain and livestock were preferred over the preoccupation with tobacco in southern Maryland. Flour, whiskey, and hides were prominent exports.

Today's visitor can feel the presence of the past in Ellicott City, the charming child of Ellicott Mills (1830). Shops filled with crafts, memorabilia, and home-baked goods are nested in original buildings of the old mill town. Samples of Americana are sold at New Market, "The Antique Capitol of Maryland." Gentle grades yield to the encroaching climbs of the Piedmont region en route to the small scenic towns of Middletown and Mount Airy.

Follow the path of the Civil War to Antietam where the scene is virtually unchanged since the battle. For more Civil War history, visit Harper's Ferry, site of John Brown's notorious raid.

Smooth, uninterrupted driving on I-70 west will deliver you easily to our day trips, but you may welcome the opportunity to drive the back roads into the history of western Maryland and West Virginia.

"Tongue Row" in Ellicott City, Maryland

W E S T

Day Trip 1

ELLICOTT CITY, MD.
MOUNT AIRY, MD.
NEW MARKET, MD.

ELLICOTT CITY, MD.

Three Quaker brothers founded this town about 1772 on the Patapsco River and made it one of the greatest milling and manufacturing towns in the East during its heyday. Later, the town became the location of an ironworks and, most importantly, the first terminus for the B&O Railroad.

While the town's adjacency to the river was a boon to local industry, flooding over the years has destroyed many of the town's historic buildings. Those that remain include the stone buildings along **Tongue Row,** which now house specialty shops; the **Colonial Inn and Opera House,** which is reported to be the site where John Wilkes Booth made his debut; **Disney's Tavern** (1790); **Mount Ida** (1828), the last home built by an Ellicott; and the former **Patapsco Hotel,** a popular lodging facility during the development of the B&O Railroad.

From Baltimore, take US-40 west to Rogers Avenue southeast (M-99) for 1 mile to Old Frederick Road. Turn left on Old Frederick Road, which becomes Main Street in Ellicott City.

WHERE TO GO

Ellicott City B&O Railroad Station Museum. Maryland Avenue and Main Street. Begin your visit at this 1831 building, which was the first terminus of the first railroad in the United States. Today, the station serves as a museum of railroad memorabilia and an information center where visitors can see a sight-and-sound show and a working model train display and browse in a gift shop. Fee. (301) 992-2344.

Tongue Row. This quaint street in mid-town, just off Main Street, is lined with original stone homes. Today it is the site of interesting specialty shops and seasonal crafts exhibits.

Walking Tour. A brochure describes a self-guided walking tour of the city's historic district. It is distributed by many area merchants and at the Howard County Tourist Information Center, Court House Drive. Free. (301) 992-2344.

Delft Gallery. Maryland Avenue and St. Paul Street. Located in the heart of the historic district, this gallery features handpainted earthenware and tiles. Delftwares and tiles depict such subjects as landscapes, seascapes, flowers and windmills as fine examples of an art that originated in Holland. Appropriately priced. Open Monday through Sunday. (301) 465-4220.

WHERE TO EAT

Cacao Lane Restaurant. 8066 Main Street. This popular restaurant located in the heart of the historic district features consistently good food, served attractively, in a friendly atmosphere. Cuisine is American and Continental. It is open seven days a week, year-round. The manager recommends reservations for parties greater than four persons. Lunch, $; dinner, $$; ☐. (301) 461-1378.

MOUNT AIRY, MD.

Located in the rich, fertile tracts of land in Frederick County's wine region, Mount Airy is a tiny rural town with a traditional Main Street. To get there from Ellicott City, return to Old Frederick Road via Main Street, take a short shunt on US-40 west, and pick up M-144 west (Frederick Road) for a scenic approach. For a more time-efficient route, remain on US-40 west until it runs concurrent with I-70 west. Continue on this route to Mount Airy's Main Street. Turn right and drive northbound into the town.

WHERE TO GO

Berrywine Plantations. 13608 Glisans Mill Road. From Main Street drive west on Prospect Road and continue on to Jacobs Road. Turn right on Woodville Road, and drive north to Glisans Mill Road. This 230-acre plantation is a family-run business founded in 1971. The first plantings of French hybrid grapes were begun in 1972. Today Berrywine features French and Italian styles of red and rosé wines, as well as German-style white wines. In addition, semi-sweet table and dessert wines are available. Besides the fine wines, the plantation offers a magnificent view of the Catoctin Mountains toward Camp David in Thurmont.

There is a gift shop on the premises, and picnic facilities are available. Open year-round; closed Wednesdays and some holidays. Guided tours available. Free. (301) 662-8687.

WEST

NEW MARKET, MD.

The Historic District of New Market is a fine example of a small town of the late Federal period. In New Market, dubbed "The Antique Capital of Maryland," the tree-shaded main street and a few of the side streets, boast more than 40 antiques, crafts, and specialty shops. Merchants offer everything from candles and doll house furniture to country crafts and period antiques. All shops are open year-round. For tours and information, call (301) 865-3318.

Continue west on US-40 from Mount Airy to New Market at the junction of M-75.

New Market Days is an annual celebration scheduled in late September. It includes good country food, buggy rides, historical displays, and entertainment. Free. For more information about this specific event, call Frank Shaw in New Market at (301) 831-6010. Or write to Mr. Shaw c/o New Market, Maryland, 21774. (See Festival and Celebration listing at back of book.)

For return routing to Baltimore, drive east on M-144 to US-40 east near Ellicott City, and follow this road to Baltimore. If you have time, you might want to continue northwest on M-144 and pick up I-70/US-40 west into Frederick for the first stop in Day Trip 2 of this section.

Ellicott City B&O Railroad Station

WEST

Day Trip 2

FREDERICK, MD.
LILY PONS, MD.
SUGAR LOAF MOUNTAIN, MD.

FREDERICK, MD.

Founded in 1745 by English and German settlers, this delightful town was originally called Fredericktown. As a frontier town it served the wagon trains that traveled through the surrounding fertile farmland on their way West across the mountains. Frederick has a wealth of historic points. From Baltimore take US-40 west to I-70/US-40 west directly to Frederick.

WHERE TO GO

Visitor Center. 19 E. Church Street. Information regarding the guided, one-and-a-half-hour walking tours originating at the Visitor Center is available here. Fee for tours. Children under 12, free. General visitor information is also available. Free. Open daily except Jan. 1 and Dec. 25. (301) 663-8703.

Barbara Fritchie House. 154 W. Patrick Street. This is a reconstruction of the home of the ardent Unionist, Barbara Fritchie. The story is told that the 95-year-old patriot dauntlessly waved her Union flag as Stonewall Jackson and his troops marched through town in 1862. According to the classic Civil War poem by John Greenleaf Whittier, she challenged him not to harm a hair on her old gray head!

Today the home rests on its original site and contains articles of historical interest. Open to the public Mondays, Wednesdays, and weekends. Fee. Discounts to children under 12 and, of course, to citizens over 60 (Barbara would have liked it that way). (301) 663-3833.

Schifferstadt. 1110 Rosemont Avenue. Constructed about 1756, this structure is a fine example of the cultural heritage of this town and the early building methods. Exhibits of arts and crafts are on display here. Open daily April 1 through December 23; closed Easter and Thanksgiving. Free. (301) 663-1611

Mount Olivet Cemetery. Located at the end of Market Street, this cemetery is the final resting place of such noted Americans as Francis Scott Key and his wife, as well as Barbara Fritchie and more than 400 Confederate soldiers from the battles of Antietam and Monocacy. Also buried here is Thomas Johnson, Maryland's first governor. Open to the public.

Rose Hill Manor Children's Museum. 1611 N. Market Street. Originally the home of Maryland's first governor, Thomas Johnson, the house (1790), carriages, and garden are restored to show 19th-century family life. Hands-on displays delight the children, and guide service is available. Free. (301) 694-1648.

WHERE TO EAT

Beckley's Family Restaurant. US-15, just 2 miles north of Frederick. Home-cooked meals, prepared to order, include pan-fried chicken, homemade soup, desserts, and pies. Beckley's serves breakfast, lunch, and dinner. $-$$; ☐. (301) 662-2126.

Red Horse Steak House. Located at the junction of US-40 and US-15 in Frederick, this restaurant's apple-red horse atop the building is a local landmark. The Red Horse specializes in steaks, fresh seafood, and prime ribs. Dinner is served seven days a week. Breakfast is served in the Coffee Shop in the adjoining motel. $$; ☐. (301) 663-3030.

LILY PONS, MD.

Located in the beautiful countryside of Frederick County, this destination is for the nature lover and curiosity seeker alike. Leave Frederick on M-355 south. Pass over I-70 to M-85 south, which is Buckeystown Pike. After passing Buckeystown, drive 3 miles to Lily Pons Road. Turn left and drive east across the Monacacy River to the fish hatchery and water gardens.

Lilypons Water Gardens. Lily Pons Road, Lily Pons. This site is one of the largest suppliers of ornamental fish and aquatic plants in the world. Lilies are in bloom from late May through August. The water garden is named after Metropolitan Opera star Miss Lily Pons, who visited the site. Free. (301) 874-5133.

WEST

SUGAR LOAF MOUNTAIN, MD.

This mountain is within 3,000 acres of privately owned countryside known as Stronghold. The estate was deeded to the Stronghold Corporation by its owner, Gordon Strong, to provide a natural preserve for the public to enjoy. More than 100,000 visitors come to Stronghold each year.

From Lilypons Water Gardens, continue east on Lily Pons Road to Park Mills Road. Turn left and drive northeast to Mount Ephraim Road. Turn right and drive southeast to Comus Road, which is within the Sugar Loaf Mountain Natural Area.

WHERE TO GO

Sugar Loaf Mountain. Early settlers gave the mountain its name because its shape reminded them of this household staple. Sugar Loaf rises 1,281 feet above the surrounding countryside. Lookouts were placed on its slopes during the Civil War. Today, visitors may stop at several lookout points carved into the natural surroundings to view the farmland of Montgomery County, the Potomac River and Frederick valleys, and the Catoctin and Blue Ridge mountains.

Hiking and picnicking are the favored activities here. Open daily. Closed December and January. Free.

Return routing to Baltimore through lovely Frederick County, at the end of this day trip, offers glimpses of valley vistas, seasonal foliage, and country communities. Return to Park Mills Road and turn right. Continue to drive northwest until you reach Fingerboard Road (M-80). Turn right and drive east, toward Urbana, and follow this route to Fountain Mills. Turn left and drive north on M-75 to New Market. Stop here for refreshment, or continue on to Baltimore via M-144 east or I-70/US-40 east.

W E S T

Day Trip 3

HAGERSTOWN, MD.
BOONSBORO, MD.
SHARPSBURG, MD.
MIDDLETOWN, MD.

HAGERSTOWN, MD.

Settlers first came to this area as a part of the movement west. In 1739, a German immigrant named Jonathan Hager settled here with his wife, Elizabeth. He called this site Hager's Delight and went on to found Elizabethtown in 1762. Later on, the two sites were officially established as Hagerstown. Today, many of the existing structures are reminders of the life and times of the 18th and 19th centuries.

Although the destinations in this day trip are relatively far from Baltimore, time-efficient routing will get you there fast. From Baltimore, take US-40 west to I-70 west to Exit 32 northwest into Hagerstown. From the Exit 32 cloverleaf, the main thoroughfare into town is US-40 west.

WHERE TO GO

Hagerstown City Park. Virginia Avenue. Rated the second most beautiful natural city park in the nation, this spot is a welcoming oasis to visitors. It features quiet picnic areas, beautifully flowered and wooded park areas, and a lake graced by majestic swans. Open year round. Free.

Washington County Museum of Fine Arts. Located within the Hagerstown City Park, this stately Georgian brick museum overlooks the park lake. It houses a permanent collection of fine arts that showcases the American School. Free; donations accepted. (301) 739-5727.

Hager House and Museum. Key Street, City Park. Built in 1739 by the town founder, Jonathan Hager, this stone residence is unique. It was constructed over a spring, so that during an Indian attack the family would not be cut off from their water supply. The museum includes 18th-century artifacts excavated on the site. Fee. (301) 797-8782.

Miller House Museum and the Valley Store Museum. 135 W. Washington Street. The Washington County Historical Society Headquarters and an information center are located in this Federal period home. Special exhibits are featured each month and include an extensive collection of dolls, antique clocks, C&O Canal memorabilia, and Civil War artifacts.

The Valley Store Museum, in the basement, is a reconstruction of a country store, complete with merchandise authentic to the years spanning 1840 to 1918. Fee. (301) 797-8782.

WHERE TO EAT

The Fez. 770 Robinwood Drive, Hagerstown. Enjoy a relaxed atmosphere, good steaks, specialty sandwiches, fresh salad bar, and homemade soups. $; no ☐. (301) 739-1244.

Del-Mar Inn Restaurant. Three miles west of Hagerstown on US-40 near I-70. The good food at reasonable prices includes chicken, spaghetti, seafood, and pizza. Open 24 hours a day; 7 days a week. This friendly stop features breakfast served "any time." $-$$; no ☐. (301) 733-2898.

BOONSBORO, MD.

Settled in 1774 by George and William Boone, who were said to have been related to the more famous Daniel, this town prospered in the 1830s when the National Pike was alive with westward moving traffic. During the Civil War, battles were fought in nearby areas by such famous Americans as Stonewall Jackson and J.E.B. Stuart.

From Frederick Street in Hagerstown, drive south onto the Old National Pike. This is also designated Alternate US-40. This route traverses farmlands and scenic valleys with vistas of Catoctin and South mountains as it brings you directly into Boonsboro.

WHERE TO GO

Boonsborough Museum of History. 113 N. Main Street. Exhibits include Civil War relics, historical weapons, Indian artifacts, and early Boonsborough memorabilia. Fee. (301) 432-6969 or 432-5151.

Crystal Grottoes Caverns. Exit Boonsboro, southwest, on M-34 for 1 mile to the caverns. Underground limestone wonders are the result of millions of years of chemical and mineral action. Born of nature and sculpted by man, these corridors of stalagmites and stalactites depict mythological and modern beings. Guided tours available. Open year-round. Fee. (301) 432-6336.

Washington Monument State Park. Return to Boonsboro and drive

WEST

south for a short distance on Alternate US-40 to the Washington Monument State Park. Besides general natural beauty, the main attraction in this park is the Washington Monument. It was erected in one day by the citizens of Boonsboro on July 4, 1827, and was the first monument built in the memory of George Washington. For the hardier visitors, the monument can be reached by walking ¼ mile uphill from the ample parking lot. Free. (301) 432-8065.

WHERE TO EAT

Adam's Auction House Restaurant. Located on Alternate US-40, just 1 mile west of Boonsboro. This restaurant serves breakfast, lunch, and dinner and features chicken, country ham, steaks, and seafood. Specialties include a Wednesday Chickey-Fry and a Friday Fish-Fry with seconds "on the house." Homemade soups and sandwiches are also worth the visit. Open all week. $-$$; □. (301) 733-6445.

Old South Mountain Inn. Located on Alternate US-40 across from the entrance to Washington Monument State Park, this historic stone inn dates back to 1730. Early American atmosphere and reliably well prepared meals are featured. Children's menu available. Closed Mondays and Christmas. $$; □. (301) 432-6155.

SHARPSBURG, MD.

The Battle of Antietam (or Sharpsburg) on Sept. 17, 1862, climaxed the first of Confederate Gen. Robert E. Lee's two attempts to carry the war into the North. Some 41,000 Southerners were pitted against the 87,000-man Federal Army of the Potomac under Gen. George B. McClellan. When the fighting ended, the course of the Civil War had been greatly altered.

It is said that more men were killed or wounded here on that infamous date in 1862 than on any other single day of the Civil War. Federal losses were 12,410; Confederate losses were 10,700. Although neither side gained a decisive victory, Lee's failure to carry the war effort effectively into the North caused Great Britain to postpone recognition of the Confederate government. The battle also gave President Abraham Lincoln the opportunity to issue the Emancipation Proclamation, which, on Jan. 1, 1863, declared free all slaves in states still in rebellion against the United States. Henceforth the war had a dual purpose; to preserve the Union and to end slavery.

From Alternate US-40, just south of Boonsboro, take M-34 Southwest (Shepherdstown Pike) through Keedysville to Sharpsburg.

WHERE TO GO

Antietam National Battlefield. From M-34 (Main Street) in Sharpsburg, travel east to M-65 (Hagerstown Pike). Turn left and drive north to

Bloody Lane, Antietam National Battlefield

the entrance of the battlefield. The Battle of Antietam was fought over an area of 12 square miles and consisted of three basic phases: morning, mid-day, and afternoon. Before touring the battlefield, go to the Visitors Center where exhibits and an 18-minute slide program provide an introduction to the Maryland campaign. Especially impressive is the panoramic view of the battlefield, complete with explanation of battle strategies. Information regarding driving tours is available here. Free.

Other stops along the tour include **Bloody Lane,** the site where the greatest number of fatalities occurred, and **Burnside Bridge,** named for the Union general whose troops attempted to cross the bridge during the battle. The **Dunkard Church** (c. 1852) was used as a makeshift fort by the Confederate army and was badly riddled by shot and shell by the Federal forces. It was rebuilt in 1863.

The battlefield is on the National Register of Historic Places. The park has a picnic area. Fishing is permitted in Antietam Creek; a Maryland fishing license is required. Relic hunting within the park is prohibited. Open year-round. Free. (301) 432-5124.

C&O Canal National Historic Park Headquarters. Located a

WEST

short distance west of Sharpsburg on M-34, just before the James Rumsey Bridge. The park administrative offices and an informed, helpful staff offer brochures on area attractions and specific information regarding the C&O Canal. Free. (301) 739-4200.

Ranger Station. Canal Road. The station is located in the immediate area of the park headquarters. Convenient free parking gives the inquiring visitor ample time to pick up maps of the C&O Canal and general park information. Take advantage of the towpath access here to enjoy a stroll along the historic canal. Free. (301) 739-6179.

From Sharpsburg, return via M-34 east to Alternate US-40 south. Turn right onto the Old National Pike to Middletown.

MIDDLETOWN, MD.

Middletown is an immaculately clean community with charming "Americana" houses. It has an air of old-fashioned comfort and homestead pride.

Several Civil War skirmishes in the vicinity crowded Middletown homes and churches with wounded soldiers. Young Nancy Crouse, a Middletown resident, is said to have wrapped the Union flag around her when the Confederate troops galloped into town. Unfortunately, Southern gallantry was at an all-time low point, and the flag was torn from her body and destroyed.

Settled in the 18th century by people of English and German descent, the town was incorporated in 1833. Today, visitors pause to appreciate this picture-postcard town and to eat the homemade ice cream from the little shop on Main Street. For day trip drivers, it marks a pleasant conclusion to a busy day.

When departing Middletown for return routing to Baltimore, continue southeast on Alternate US-40 into Frederick. Here, you can take M-144 east to US-40 east, or take I-70/US-40 east into Baltimore.

If you choose to extend your day trip while still in Sharpsburg, continue southwest on M-34 into Shepherdstown, the first destination in Day Trip 4 of this chapter.

W E S T

Day Trip 4

SHEPHERDSTOWN, WEST VA.
HARPERS FERRY, WEST VA.
Worth More Time:
CHARLES TOWN, WEST VA.

SHEPHERDSTOWN, WEST VA.

Shepherdstown was charted in 1764, and early settlers reached it by traveling south from York to Lancaster, Pennsylvania, on the "Old Philadelphia Wagon Road." Most of these early settlers were of German descent, with a sprinkling of English, Scottish, and Dutch families.

Among their ranks were potters, smiths, and other craftsmen, as well as merchants and industrialists who gave the town an economic base. One such entrepreneur was James Rumsey, who invented and successfully demonstrated the operation of his steam-powered boat on the Potomac River here on Dec. 3, 1787. The town flourished during the 18th and 19th centuries with the Town Run providing the power to turn the wheels of its industry.

Because of its strategic location, 4 miles south of Antietam Battlefield and 10 miles west of Harpers Ferry, Shepherdstown saw much activity during the Civil War. At the time of the Battle of Antietam, the town became a huge field hospital sheltering wounded Confederate soldiers.

Shepherdstown also played an important part in the history of the C&O Canal. Directly across the Potomac River from Canal Lock # 38 are the remains of the dock and warehouse area of the town. From there, Canal barges loaded with farm products were poled across the river to enter the canal through the Shepherdstown Lock and continued to markets in Georgetown and Alexandria, Va.

Today, visitors enjoy driving through this quiet, country town to sense the presence of its history, especially in the downtown area, which has

WEST

been designated a historical district on the National Register.

From Baltimore, take US-40 west to I-70 west. Then take Exit 49 off of I-70, just outside Frederick. From here, pick up Alternate US-40 west (south of Boonsboro). Then follow M-34 west across the Potomac River to nearby Shepherdstown.

WHERE TO GO

James Rumsey Monument. At the north end of Mill Street stands the commemorative obelisk dedicated to the industrial genius of James Rumsey, who gave the first public demonstration of the steamboat in 1787.

Shepherd Grist Mill. Mill and High streets, Shepherdstown. The mill was constructed in 1739 by Thomas Shepherd, founder of Shepherdstown. With a diameter of 40 feet, the overshot waterwheel is said to be one of the world's largest. Today, it is privately owned. While it is not open for tours, take the opportunity while shopping in the High Street district to walk by it.

O'Hurley's General Store. 205 East Washington Street. This sprawling country store features homestead supplies such as sleds, glassware, dry goods, cast-iron cookware, crockery, and coffins. A colorful brochure lists more of their inventory: enamelware, fruit presses, baskets, and dinner bells. If this colorful combination intrigues you, you might want to accept the following invitation from this family-run establishment: "Homesteaders, housewives and others wishing our circular will be furnished same by sending us their address." (304) 876-6907.

WHERE TO EAT

Bavarian Inn and Lodge. From Shepherdstown, this property is 1 mile north on WV-480 at the west end of the Potomac River Bridge. The award-winning Bavarian Inn and Lodge is West Virginia's top rated country inn and restaurant. Beautiful guestrooms, some with fireplaces, overlook the Potomac River. The restaurant features fine German cuisine and serves breakfast, lunch, and dinner. Wild game and other specialties are served in season. Children's menu is available. Reservations are advised. $$-$$$; ☐. (304) 876-2551.

Yellow Brick Bank Restaurant. German and Princess streets, Shepherdstown. A corner bank was transformed into this colorful restaurant which features an excellent, varied menu served in a charming atmosphere that is sure to please. Open year-round. An excellent Sunday brunch is served. Reservations are recommended. $$; ☐. (304) 876-2208.

HARPERS FERRY, WEST VA.

Harpers Ferry, situated on a point of land at the confluence of the Shenandoah and Potomac rivers and dominated by the Blue Ridge Mountains, was a beckoning wilderness in the early 1700s. By mid-19th century it was a town of some 3,000 inhabitants, an important arms-producing center, and a transportation link between east and west. John Brown's raid in 1859 and the Civil War thrust the town into national prominence. The destruction wrought by the war and repeated flooding were responsible for the town's eventual decline.

The first settler on this land was Peter Stephens, a trader, who came here in 1733 and set up a primitive ferry service at the junction of the two rivers. Fourteen years later, Robert Harper, a millwright and the man for whom the town is named, settled here, taking over Stephen's ferry operation. Seeing the water power potential, he later built a mill. The ferry and the mill have long since disappeared.

Within a century, Harpers Ferry developed from a tiny village into an industrialized community. Then came disaster. In October, 1859, John Brown's abolitionist raid jarred the peaceful town. The Civil War that followed 17 months later left a path of destruction that wrecked the town's economy. The armory and arsenal buildings were burned in 1861 to keep them from falling into Confederate hands. Because of the town's location and its railway system, Union and Confederate troops frequently moved through Harpers Ferry, and soldiers of both armies occupied the town intermittently throughout the war.

The largest military operation against Harpers Ferry occurred prior to the Battle of Antietam in September of 1862 when Confederate forces under Gen. Stonewall Jackson seized the town and captured the 12,700-man Union garrison commanded by Col. Dixon Miles.

Discouraged by continual war damage and the lack of employment, many townspeople moved away. For years afterward, empty buildings stood in silent desolation, and once-active industrial sites were slowly reclaimed by nature.

The one bright hope in the story of Harpers Ferry after the Civil War was the establishment of a normal school for the education of freed blacks. The first classroom of what was to become Storer College was located in the Lockwood House, an abandoned armory dwelling above the town. The college remained in operation until 1955.

Today Harpers Ferry stands as a living museum describing the actions of a man whose words and deeds prophesied the advent of the Civil War.

Harpers Ferry National Historical Park is a remarkable restoration of a time and events in America's history. It offers 23 points of interest

WEST

within and around the area. The park entrance is located on US-340 at Shenandoah Street.

WHERE TO GO

Visitors Center. Located on Shenandoah Street near High Street. Begin your visit to the park with an introductory slide program and exhibits on the park themes. Information on self-guided and conducted walking tours is also available here. Most of the theme activities in the park are during the summer months, when costumed guides explain the significance of points of interest.

In the fall and spring, park activities are restricted to weekends, but the Center and some historic buildings remain open. Picnicking and camping are permitted in the immediate area. Call the Visitors Center for details. For information, write the Park Superintendent, Box 65, Harpers Ferry, WV, 25425. Open all year, except Christmas and New Year's Day. Free. (304) 535-6371.

A word about John Brown. John Brown, 1800-1859, was the man whose raid brought Harpers Ferry to national attention. An ardent abolitionist, he fixed upon Harpers Ferry as the starting point for the insurrection against slavery. Brown and his 22-man "army of liberation" attacked the town on the night of Oct. 16, 1859, seizing the armory and several other strategic points. They were captured, brought to trial for murder and treason, and hanged on Dec. 2, 1859. On the day of his execution, Brown prophesied that the crimes of society could only be purged by bloodshed. Sixteen months later, on April 12, 1861, the war that John Brown seemed to foretell began at a place called Fort Sumter in Charleston Harbor, South Carolina.

Harpers Ferry Tour

Begin your tour of Harpers Ferry at High Street, located 1 block past the Visitors Center. This becomes the main street of the historic district. Many sites and shops located on High Street are ones that you will want to visit. No numerical designations assign addresses to these sites, but you'll easily find them as you walk, beginning at Shenandoah Street, along High Street. As High Street leaves the immediate historic district, it becomes Washington Street. Thus, sites indicated on Washington Street are actually located on an extension of High Street. The town is small. Patience and a good pair of comfortable shoes will take you wherever you might want to go.

Historic Sites

Primarily relating to the events surrounding John Brown's raid and the Civil War that followed, sites include: the **Harper House,** c. 1755, the oldest structure in the park; **Arsenal Square,** the foundations of the two U.S. Arsenal buildings that were burned when Federal troops evacuated the town at the beginning of the Civil War; **John Brown's Fort,** the Armory firehouse used as a refuge by the famous abolitionist; the

WEST

John Brown Museum, a restored building which houses a theater and museum relating the events of the famous raid; and the **Civil War Museum,** where exhibits tell the story of the effects of the war on Harpers Ferry and its citizens.

Other Attractions

John Brown Wax Museum. High Street, Harpers Ferry. This attraction provides a colorful, life-size exhibit of the story of John Brown's famous raid. Fee. (304) 535-6342.

Blue Ridge Outfitters. Located 4 miles southwest of Harpers Ferry on US-340. Half-day raft trips on the Potomac River begin just below Great Falls, where visitors paddle through spectacular Mather Gorge, a narrow, mile-long canyon with sheer 40-to-60-foot rock walls and continuous rolling waves. A picnic lunch is scheduled on an island mid-river. Blue Ridge Outfitters says this is an ideal trip for beginners and veteran rafters alike through one of the most beautiful recreation areas of the East.

Trips are limited to ages 10 through 60. Fee. Reservations are required. Write to Blue Ridge Outfitters, P.O. Box 456, Harpers Ferry, WV, 25425. Or call (304) 725-3444.

WHERE TO EAT

Mountain House Cafe. High Street, Harpers Ferry; located in the 15th property west of Shenandoah Street. This sidewalk cafe, in a beautiful setting, features home-cooked, country-style food plus light fare salads and sandwiches. Open year-round. $; no □. (304) 535-2339.

Hilltop House. Ridge Street, Harpers Ferry. Drive west on High Street until it becomes Washington Street. At the intersection of Columbia and Washington streets, turn right. Drive to Ridge Street and turn right again. Follow Ridge Street to its dead end in a cul-de-sac at the Hilltop House.

Once the retreat of President Woodrow Wilson, Mark Twain, and Dr. Alexander Graham Bell, the restored Hilltop House overlooks the junction of the Potomac and Shenandoah rivers and three states. Both dining and lodging are afforded here. Specialties include Southern fried chicken, baked ham, stuffed flounder, and an all-day buffet on weekends. Open year-round except at Christmas through New Year's. $$; no □. (304) 535-6321.

WHERE TO SHOP

Sleepy Hollow Creations. High Street; four properties west of Shenandoah Street. West Virginia crafts, including unique candleholders, planters, and lamps sculpted from tin cans and other metals, are on sale here. A free catalog is available by mailing your request to P.O. Box 247, Harpers Ferry, WV, 25425. (304) 535-2354.

Mountaineer Jewelry and Gem Manufacturing Company. High Street; 12 properties west from Shenandoah Street. This is an unusual jewelry manufacturing and outlet store. Its primary products are sterling silver and gold-filled jewelry, as well as semi-precious and precious stones. Custom work, cut stones, jewelry parts, pewter, and West Virginia coal carvings are available. (304) 535-2372.

Westwind Potters. High Street; 13th property west from Shenandoah Street. Fine handcrafted porcelain and stoneware objects for daily use are among the fascinating display of goods here. Some are produced right in the retail shop. See expert potters creating vases, mugs, bowls, pitchers, honey pots, and other fun and functional items. All wares are lead-free, as well as oven, dishwasher, and microwave safe. Commissions and mail orders are accepted by writing to P.O. Box 686, Harpers Ferry, WV, 25425. (304) 535-2511.

Patches, Inc. 1499 Washington Street, Harpers Ferry. All quilting needs can be met in this shop. More than 1,000 bolts of calico, mini-prints, solids, blends, ginghams, and chintz are here. Also available are stencils, templates, and patchwork accessories. If you're not a "pro" but would like to learn, there are books on quilt making in this shop. Some merchants take a hiatus during the Christmas holidays, so call ahead for more specific hours. (304) 535-6968.

WORTH MORE TIME

Charles Town and the **Charles Town Races** are located in the Shenandoah Valley, just 6 miles west of Harpers Ferry on US-340 in the eastern panhandle of West Virginia. Driving time is just outside our two-hour perimeter, but you may want to gather a group of friends to enjoy a day of thoroughbred racing at this beautiful track. Top off your day with convenient dining at the Skyline Terrace for a spectacular view from the terraced tables. Expenses for the day will include admission to the track and parking. Closed Mondays and Tuesdays. From Baltimore the toll-free number is 685-0200. For Washington, the toll-free number is 737-2323. From all other areas, call (304) 725-7001.

NORTHWEST

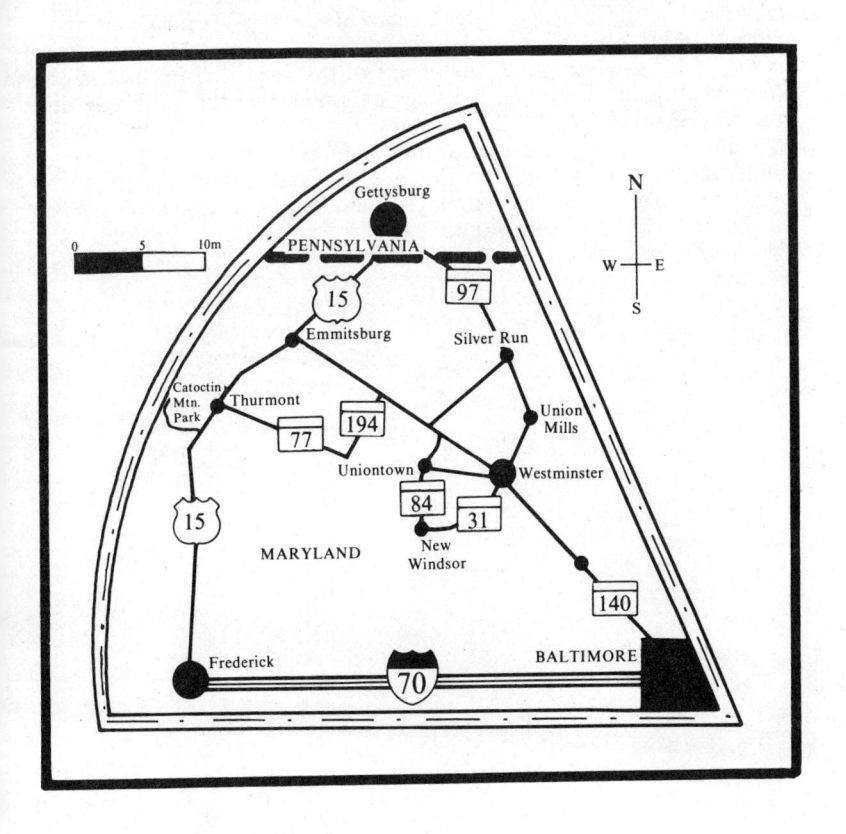

NORTHWEST

Travel northwest to stately mansions, picturesque farmhouses, and the birthplace of Francis Scott Key. Explore 200 years of town and farm life while revisiting the Revolutionary and Civil War eras. Picture yourself in a Currier and Ives setting replete with indigenous brick-end barns.

The farmland in the northwest corridor is perhaps the most fertile in Maryland. Corn, wheat, barley, and hay fields stretch for miles over the gently rolling hills. Rich farmlands, coupled with agribusiness, set the scene for past and present lifestyles. The Carroll County Farm Museum together with the Union Mills Homestead and Grist Mill are living museums touting the central significance of the farm, its fields, and the mills. Family life was sustained by these rich tracts of land. And, for some, it was ended at Gettysburg, site of one of the most decisive battles of American history. Civil War buffs come from all over the world to visit this battlefield shrine.

Amid the natural beauty and historic treasures of the Catoctin Mountains lies Thurmont, home of Camp David and mountain retreat of America's presidents. A swing through Emmitsburg takes you to the home of the first American born-saint, Elizabeth Ann Seton, as we reach the two-hour perimeter of the northwest tours.

Union Mills Homestead, Union Mills, Maryland

NORTHWEST

Day Trip 1

REISTERSTOWN, MD.
WESTMINSTER, MD.
UNIONTOWN, MD.
NEW WINDSOR, MD.

REISTERSTOWN, MD.

Begin this day trip to the northwest corridor in Reisterstown. Although little has been preserved of its Revolutionary era, the town retains some original buildings on Main Street. Today, these structures house specialty and antique shops. From Baltimore, drive northwest on M-140 (Reisterstown Road) to reach this quaint destination.

Reisterstown was founded on a tract of land called "Reister's Desire" in 1758 by a German immigrant and innkeeper, John Reister. Just north of Reister's inn and blacksmith shop, the town grew and became a significant stopping point for travelers. The road that stretched from Baltimore to Gettysburg and Hanover, Pennsylvania, traversed this settlement and gave rise to such businesses as Forney's Tavern, known for its hospitality and good food. While the road brought prosperity, to some it foretold times of growth and change. In 1804, Jacob Medairy sought to block this progress by constructing a house in its path. Roadbuilders simply diverted around the house, and this deflection has been preserved over time. Look for it at the junction of Reisterstown Road (M-140) and Cockeys Mill Road.

Progress continued to take precedence over preservation as new houses, gas stations, and businesses were constructed in this busy corridor. Despite the low profile of the town's historic beginnings, there remains a sense of its presence. At the bend in the road is **Beckley's Blacksmith Shop** and the **Polly Reister House;** a two-and-a-half-story brick building with a one-story wing, erected in 1779. The **Henry Weist House** is located at 410 Main Street. Erected in 1773, it is constructed of stone and stucco and is indicative of the architectural style of the local area. Returning to Cockeys Mill Road, drive a short distance to the **Reisterstown Cemetery**. Originally developed around a log cabin that was used for Lutheran religious services as early as 1765, it is the resting place for early town residents and local soldiers and patriots of the Revolutionary War.

WESTMINSTER, MD.

William Winchester, an English immigrant, bought more than 100 acres of land in 1754 for 150 pounds or about $4.50 per acre. Later, he named the property Westminster in memory of his British birthplace. The town quickly became a trading center for the bounty from the rich surrounding farmland and a stopping-off point for wagons traveling between the grain fields of central Pennsylvania and the Port of Baltimore. When Carroll County was created in 1837, the city's central location and its zealous advocates helped secure its designation as the county seat.

The strategic location and bountiful resources of Westminster lent themselves well to the needs of the Union and Confederate troops during the Civil War. Both forces occupied the town three times within three years. Although the town was active in supplying resources, no significant battle action occurred here. The town, suffering little, returned easily to peacetime activities.

Westminster remains a peaceful, country town which is truly a pleasure to visit. Many of its fine buildings are included in the National Register of Historic Places. The Town Center is charming with its preserved 18th-century homes. Today's visitors will delight in the variety of specialty shops among the historic sites.

From Reisterstown continue northeast on M-140 to Westminster.

WHERE TO GO

Walking Tours. 210 E. Main Street. Stop first at the Visitors Information Center to pick up literature on local attractions and specific information on the Walking Tours. The **Court Street and Court Square Walking Tour**'s theme is that of planned city development coupled respectfully with preservation of the old. The tour incorporates examples of early American architecture, an 1846 Episcopal Church and graveyard, the 1837 Old Jail, and the Pennsylvania-Georgian-style courthouse. The tour takes approximately one hour. Free. (301) 848-1388.

The Early Country Architecture Walking Tour of Westminster incorporates a variety of architectural styles and interesting facades, and it can be extended to take in the downtown shopping area. The tour takes approximately one and one-half hours. Free. (301) 848-1388.

NORTHWEST

While both of these self-guided walking tours are free, arrangements for guided tours for groups of 10 or more may be arranged for a reasonable fee.

The county Office of Promotion and Tourism welcomes your requests for additional information at (301) 848-4500 or by writing to 225 N. Center Street, Westminster, MD, 21157. While visiting the county information center in Westminster, be sure to pick up the walking tour guide for Uniontown—the next destination in this county on our day trip itinerary.

Kimmey House. 210 E. Main Street. Having begun your visit to Westminster at the Visitors Center, you are already standing in this c. 1800 town house which also serves as the headquarters of the Historical Society of Carroll County. The Kimmey House contains administrative offices, a genealogical research library, **Miss Carroll's Childrens Shop** (a permanent doll and toy exhibit), a gift shop, and an auditorium for lectures and receptions. Fee. (301) 848-6494.

Shellman House. 206 E. Main Street. In 1807, Jacob Sherman, who migrated from Pennsylvania, purchased one of the original lots laid out in 1764 by William Winchester, founder of Westminster. On that site he built a Flemish bond, five-bay, two-and-one-half-story brick town house as a wedding present for his daughter, Eve. One of the oldest extant structures in Westminster, the house is representative of rural Georgian architecture and retains many of its original architectural appointments.

Now known as the Shellman House, in the 1860s it was deeded to Katherine Jones Shellman, widow of Col. James M. Shellman, first burgess of Westminster and designer of the 1838 Carroll County Court House. Their daughter, Mary Bostwick Shellman, lived there as one of the county's most colorful citizens.

From the Civil War through World War I, "Miss Mary" was active in many reform movements and was instrumental in bringing phone service to the county. She entertained Alexander Graham Bell during his visit to the town and originated Memorial Day observations here in 1868.

Today, as a historic museum, the Shellman House and its furnishings reflect the many lifestyles of people living in the 19th century. Tours are available. Fee. (301) 848-6494.

Carroll County Farm Museum. 500 S. Center Street, Westminster. The entrance is located between M-32 and M-27. If you hurry through this fascinating attraction, chances are you'll miss the bonus that comes with taking your time and soaking up the pervasive feeling of the 19th-century farming lifestyle. The main house of this living museum was built in 1852 and offers today's visitors six rooms on display with authentic furnishings.

The Museum buildings are surrounded by 140 acres of open space with a lake, picnic tables, large shade trees, and nature trails.

The area comes alive with historic functions during harvest days and festivals scheduled each year. (See Festivals and Celebrations at the back of the book.) Free parking is provided. Fee. (301) 848-7775.

WHERE TO EAT

Baugher's Country Restaurant and Farm Orchard Market. At the junction of M-31 and M-32 (Main Street) in Westminster. This combination restaurant, market, and bakery features a selection ranging from steaks to Eastern Shore seafood, plus homemade baked goods and ice cream. You can also pick your own fruits and vegetables here. $; ☐. (301) 848-7413.

The Treat Shop. Six W. Main Street. For light fare lunches, this stop is one of the best. $; ☐. (301) 848-0028 or (301) 876-6388.

Maria's Restaurant. 532 Baltimore Boulevard (M-140). Maria's features a variety of fare including seafood, steaks, pasta, and pizza. $$; ☐. (301) 848-5666 or (301) 876-2611.

Cockey's Tavern. 216 E. Main Street. Fresh seafood is the specialty here. Sample lobster, fish, and crabs at their best. Also, don't miss the homemade soups and pies. $$-$$$; ☐. (301) 848-4202.

WHERE TO SHOP

The Carroll County Farmer's Market. Located at the Carroll County Agricultural Center, Smith Avenue, in Westminster. Parking is adjacent to the Farm Museum. Be sure to sample the homemade baked goods, fresh fruits and vegetables, meats, seafood, and eggs. Other offerings include crafts, flowers, shrubs, and free weekly demonstrations by local artists. Open most Saturdays from 8 A.M. to 1 P.M. Be sure to call ahead for specific dates. (301) 875-2158 or (301) 875-2510.

The Country Store. 500 S. Center Street. The proprietors of this shop at the Carroll County Farm Museum extend the invitation to come and enjoy a touch of yesteryear. Gifts, sweet treats, toys, and "necessaries" are sold. (301) 876-6688.

UNIONTOWN, MD.

This country village is one of the oldest in Carroll County, dating back to the late 18th century. It is situated on a large tract of land once known as the "Orchard." Uniontown was a prosperous business community prior to the Civil War, but when the Western Maryland Railroad bypassed Uniontown, it forged the area's future as a quiet, rural spot, untouched by commercialism.

At the west end of town, which is the oldest part, there are several large brick homes which were built in the early 1800s. These houses were the taverns and the hotel of the earlier village. Today they are preserved and occupied by private citizens of the town.

There have been few changes here since the late 19th Century. Uniontown is still the quaint, peaceful village it was then. In 1970 it was designated an Historic District.

Visitors may delight in the number of antique shops in the area. Merchants here specialize in handcrafts, antique furniture, and handmade reproductions. Be sure to visit the country store and town post office located in the center of town.

From Westminster, continue west on M-140 to Royer Road. Turn left and continue to Uniontown Road. Then, drive 6 miles on Uniontown Road to Uniontown.

WHERE TO GO

Uniontown Walking Tour. Pick up the walking tour to Uniontown at the Visitors Information Center, 210 E. Main Street, in Westminster, the second city listed in this day trips sector.

One of the oldest villages in the county, Uniontown has managed to preserve the intrinsic quality of a small, 19th-century town. The free tour of the historic district takes about one hour. A guide is available for groups of 10 or more for a reasonable fee. To get more information, to request advance walking tours by mail, or to arrange for a guided group tour, call (301) 848-4500, extension 235, or write to the Office of Tourism and Promotion, 225 N. Center Street, Westminster, MD, 21157.

NEW WINDSOR, MD.

Settled in the early 19th century, the town was formerly called Sulphur Springs. It was renamed New Windsor in 1844 and today boasts a unique International Gift Shop, one of the largest of four such non-profit outlets for artisan's crafts in the country.

From Uniontown, drive south on M-84 to New Windsor at the junction of M-31.

WHERE TO GO

The International Gift Shop. Located in the New Windsor Service Center, Main Street at M-31. Owned and operated by the World Ministries Commission, the gift shop showcases the art and quality handcrafts of more than 40 countries.

Here artisans produce attractive items using the skills of their heritage and the materials of their country. Revenues from the sale of these indigenous crafts are channeled both to the artisan and to the procurement of clothing and medical supplies for the contributing country, helping to build vital links from one culture to another.

Open daily except Sundays. A cafeteria-style dining room is on the premises. (301) 635-6464, Extension 55.

For return routing to Baltimore, drive east on M-31 to Westminster. Then drive east on M-140 to Baltimore. Or, if time permits, continue

NORTHWEST

driving west on M-140 to Emmitsburg for the first stop in Day Trip 2 of this chapter.

Carroll County Farm Museum

NORTHWEST

Day Trip 2

EMMITSBURG, MD.
THURMONT, MD.:
Catoctin Mountain National Park, Cunningham Falls State Park

EMMITSBURG, MD.

This rural community, just 11 miles south of Gettysburg, is of special interest to visitors of the Catholic faith. Tucked into the beautifully forested foothills of western Maryland is the first National Catholic Shrine in the United States: a replica of the Grotto of Lourdes. Also in Emmitsburg is the peaceful retreat of Mother Elizabeth Ann Seton—the first American-born saint. Abounding in nature's beauty and bountiful quiet areas for meditation, this Maryland landmark is a worthy, experiential venture.

From Baltimore, drive northwest on M-140 to Westminster, through Taneytown to Emmitsburg. Turn left at the town square and drive ½ mile to the Seton Shrines.

WHERE TO GO

The Seton Shrine Center. 333 S. Seton Avenue, Emmitsburg. Visitors are directed first to the Seton Shrine Center for an orientation to the self-guided tours on the "Seton Way." Visitors are requested to maintain the atmosphere of quiet retreat and meditation. A brief slide presentation highlights the historical sites at the shrine. Free. Contributions are accepted. Ample free parking and a gift shop are located nearby. (301) 447-6606.

Saint Elizabeth Ann Seton (Mother Seton) was the founder of the religious order of the Sisters of Charity and is now canonized as the first American-born saint.

Married to William Seton at the age of 20, she bore him five children. When widowed in 1803, she turned to the Catholic Church for solace and converted to Catholicism in 1805. She went on to become a nun in 1808 and opened a school in Baltimore. After receiving the title of "Mother" in 1809, she migrated to Emmitsburg where she established the order of the Sisters of Charity and the first parochial school in the United States. Mother Seton died in Emmitsburg in 1821, was Beatified in 1963, and was Canonized in 1975.

The National Shrine Grotto of Lourdes. Grotto Road, off US-15 in Emmitsburg. This tribute to the Catholic faith is the oldest replica of Lourdes Grotto in the Western Hemisphere. Stations of the cross are beautifully placed along a natural, garden path to the Grotto. Open year-round from dawn to dusk. Regularly scheduled services are held from Easter to Nov. 1 each year. (301) 447-6122.

WHERE TO EAT

Gentleman Jim's Restaurant. 200 S. Seton Avenue, Emmitsburg. The menu offers a full range of American cuisine from steaks to seafood with an abundant sandwich selection available all day. $-$$; □. (301) 447-2366.

The Palms Restaurant. 20 W. Main Street, Emmitsburg. This dining spot features old-fashioned "Ma and Pa" cooking and serves breakfast, lunch, and dinner. Nightly specials. $; no □. (301) 447-2303.

THURMONT, MD.

Thurmont is a small, rural town immediately adjacent to the Catoctin Mountain National Park and the Cunningham Falls State Park. The original settlement dates back to 1751 when the Jacob Weller family built their homestead here after abandoning a wagon train headed west. The Weller's established several small industries here, and the town became known as Mechanicstown during the early years. When the railroad was built nearby, the area became easily accessible to city folks seeking a mountain retreat. The magnificent scenery and high altitude made the area a popular resort, and it was renamed Thurmont, "gateway to the mountains."

From Emmitsburg, drive south on the Catoctin Mountain Highway (US-15) to Thurmont.

WHERE TO GO

The Catoctin Mountain Zoo. This natural attraction is located a short distance south of the town of Thurmont, on US-15, near the entrance to the Cunningham Falls State Park. Selected endangered species and exhibits of 300 animals are displayed amid green, mountainside surroundings. Special animal shows are arranged during May through September. Open

NORTHWEST

April through October. Fee. For more information regarding exhibits and special events, call (301) 271-7488.

CATOCTIN MOUNTAIN NATIONAL PARK

From Thurmont proper, drive a short distance south on US-15 to M-77. Turn right and drive west to the park entrance. Just off M-77 is the Visitors Information Center, which offers details on park programs and facilities. Adjacent to the center is a small display area which highlights the cultural and natural histories of the area and its recreational activities. The center and exhibits are free. Open daily. (301) 824-2574.

Facilities and recreational opportunities are spread among 5,769 acres of magnificent mountainside and are administered by the National Park Service. The park's name was derived from the Kittocton Indian tribe that once lived at the foot of the mountains near the Potomac River.

After picking up your free pocket map guide to the park at the visitor's center, begin your survey of things to see and do. A self-guided auto tour along 7 miles of the back roads of the Catoctin ridge begins at the intersection of Park Central Road and Manahan Road and follows a route of scenic and historic interest.

A developed picnic area is located on Owens Creek and offers modern restrooms, tables, fireplaces, and trash receptacles. Self-guiding walking trails are designated throughout the park; leaflets available at the trailheads describe nature along the routes. Hiking, cross-country skiing, and snowshoeing are readily available for the hardier visitor. About 25 miles of well-marked trails, such as Wolf Rock and Thurmont Vista, traverse the park to outstanding views and natural wonders. Parking areas are provided at the trailheads. For more specific information regarding all recreational facilities and for an advance mailing of the park guide map, call (301) 824-2574.

OF SPECIAL INTEREST

Camp David, the mountain retreat of American presidents since Franklin D. Roosevelt, is located here just off of Park Central Road. It is closed to the public.

Blue Blazes Still. Situated within walking distance from the visitor's center in the park is a genuine still which was relocated here from the Smokey Mountains after Prohibition days. It is operated by the National Park Service as an interpretative program and is open to the public from Memorial Day to Oct. 31, weekends only. Free. Sorry, no samples! (301) 663-9330.

Owens Creek Campground is open from mid-April through the third Sunday of November and features modern restrooms, tables, and fireplaces.

NORTHWEST

CUNNINGHAM FALLS STATE PARK

M-77 runs east and west, right through the middle of the Catoctin Mountain and Cunningham Falls parks. So, your visit to this area has a double bonus as you select from the scenery and fun in each park. The 4,950 acres in Cunningham Falls State Park are distributed between two separate recreation areas: the **Manor Area,** located on the park's eastern boundary near US-15, and the **William Houck Area,** located just 3 miles west of Thurmont, off M-77 on Catoctin Hollow Road. Keep these separated sites in mind so that you'll easily locate the recreational facility you choose.

The State Park office at the William Houck Area is open year-round. An information kiosk located at the Manor Area is open on weekends from April through October. Two developed picnic areas are provided at the Manor and William Houck Areas and have restrooms, tables, fireplaces, and trash receptacles. No fires are permitted when picnicking elsewhere in the park.

Two nature-oriented walking trails are the Cunningham Falls Trail and the Renaissance Trail. Descriptive leaflets are available at the trailheads. Hiking, cross-country skiing, and snowshoeing are especially good on Cat Rock Trail; there is a parking area at the trailhead.

Camping at the William Houck Campground and the Manor Campground is available from mid-April through October for families. Restrooms, tables, and fireplaces are provided.

Swimming, fishing, and boating are available on Hunting Creek Lake, which has two sandy beaches, a modern bathhouse, and a concession building. The lake is stocked with fish, and a Maryland fishing license with trout stamp is required for persons 16 years of age and older. Stream fishing in Owens Creek, Big Hunting Creek, and Little Hunting Creek is also regulated by the State of Maryland. Canoes may be rented during the summer and fall.

Cunningham Falls State Park is administered by the Maryland Park Service. Park headquarters are located at the William Houck Area. For more information regarding facilities and recreational opportunities or for an advance mailing of the park map and guide, call (301) 271-2495 or 271-7574.

OF SPECIAL INTEREST

The Catoctin Iron Furnace. Located in the southeastern tip of the Cunningham Falls State Park, on M-806 at Catoctin Hollow Road. This massive stone furnace, vintage 1771, smelted ore for shells used in the Battle of Yorktown and continued to function until 1905. The stone cottages of the original iron workers are situated nearby. Free.

NORTHWEST

From Cunningham Falls State Park, continue south on US-15 to Frederick, and explore the opportunities described in Day Trip 2 of the West section. If time doesn't permit this extended itinerary, pick up I-70 east out of Frederick to US-40 east to Baltimore. Or, simply reverse your routing on this day trip by driving northeast on US-15 into Thurmont and Emmitsburg. From Emmitsburg, drive southeast on M-140 into Baltimore.

WHERE TO EAT

Cozy Restaurant. 105 Frederick Road, Thurmont. The pride of Frederick County is this unusual restaurant with 10 dining rooms (seating capacity near 700). The well-served family fare is varied American cuisine. After 4 P.M., Monday through Friday, Cozy prepares a "groaning board" with more than 60 items plus a do-it-yourself ice cream sundae bar. Open daily. Children's menu available and sandwiches served anytime. $-$$; □. (301) 271-7373.

The Mountain Gate Family Restaurant. 141 Frederick Road, Thurmont. Excellent, homestyle cooking served in a comfortable environment. No alcoholic beverages served. $; □. (301) 271-4373.

The Shamrock Restaurant. US-15 and Fitzgerald Road, Thurmont. Excellent seafood and salad are served in a friendly manner amid the Irish decor. $-$$ □. (301) 271-2912.

WHERE TO SHOP

The Cozy Shops. Adjacent to the Cozy Restaurant are a series of quaint shops featuring another "groaning board" of items. **The General Store** at 106 Frederick Road is a linen and candy outlet, and it also offers jams and jellies, pewter, tins, candles, soaps, crafts, and much more. (301) 271-2445. **The Doll House** at 102 Frederick Road boasts dolls for all ages at all prices. (301) 271-3430. **The Cozy Antiques and Trivia Shop** at 101 Frederick Road invites you to stop and browse at your leisure among the assorted treasures. (301) 271-3245. And, **The Floral Shop** at 104 Frederick Road makes arrangements for any occasion and features a Christmas Shoppe. (301) 271-2445.

The Gateway Orchard Farm Market and Candyland. Just ½ mile north of Thurmont on US-15 is a unique combination attraction featuring farm-fresh produce all year. The proprietor recommends calling ahead for information regarding the availability of fruits or vegetables for canning or freezing. Gateway also carries more than 100 varieties of candies, as well as bulk chocolates and flavorings to make your own recipes. Open seven days a week. (301) 271-2322.

Toomey's Farm Market and Orchard. Located at the southern tip of Thurmont proper on US-15. The orchard has been in operation since the early 1930s and is known for its quality fruit. The farm market is a recent addition to the orchard and has freshly picked vegetables grown locally and in season. Some "pick-your-own" is available in the orchard.

Toomey's is a testimony to the blessings that Mother Nature bestowed on this mountainside. Fall harvests mean Applefest time: crisp, juicy apples and freshly pressed cider. Open year-round. (301) 271-7382.

Wagon Wheels Gifts. 14802 N. Franklinville Road, Thurmont. Frederick County is dotted with quaint shops with a variety of wares, and the Wagon Wheels is among the most enjoyable. Fine collectibles include porcelain dolls, music boxes, and German-made steins, along with a wide variety of kitchen items. Candles, baskets, handcrafted items, and gifts with a holiday theme are among the offerings. A special Christmas shop is featured from August through mid-January. Open daily. (301) 271-4900.

NORTHWEST

Day Trip 3

UNION MILLS, MD.
GETTYSBURG, PA.

UNION MILLS, MD.

Ah! Green grasses and golden crops woven around the contours of rolling hills. Dairy herds and horse farms tended by the dauntless vigil of endless white fences, and a friendliness that just comes "natural" to the folks who live here. Union Mills is set amid Carroll County's finest scenery. From Baltimore, drive north on Reisterstown Road (M-140). Immediately after passing Reisterstown, bear left onto the Westminster Pike (also M-140). At Westminster, turn right onto the Littlestown Pike (M-97) and drive north.

WHERE TO GO

The Union Mills Homestead. As you drive 7 miles north on M-97 from Westminster, the Homestead will be on your right. Also known as the **Shriver Homestead,** the main house is a weathered, gray clapboard dwelling facing the valley carved by Big Pipe Creek. The Homestead has been there through many stages of growth, beginning as 4 rooms in 1797. The early work of David and Andrew Shriver was soon outgrown and the homestead grew to a final 23 rooms to meet the needs of the Shriver family for a continuous six generations. Nearby, they constructed their brick grist and saw mill on Pipe Creek.

While it is doubtful that a visit to this attraction will completely convert you from occasional binges of closet cleaning, its unique fascination lies in the preserved, undisturbed, and well-utilized array of tools, toys, and furniture which spanned 150 years.

Virtually every item acquired by this family was retained and used. Seldom was anything destroyed. The antithesis of today's "disposable society," the Shriver Homestead has a dual value. It is a tribute to the days when people repaired articles rather than replacing them, and further, it is a living documentation of American farm life. This site has been declared a National Historic Landmark. Fee. Call for hours. (301) 848-2288.

For more information about the Homestead and special events here during the year, write to 3311 Littlestown Pike, Westminster, MD, 21157.

The Union Mills Grist Mill. Established adjacent to the Shriver Homestead on Big Pipe Creek, the old mill was constructed from more than 100,000 bricks that were handmade from clay found on the property. Water diverted from Big Pipe Creek powered the large undershot water wheel. In time the brick grist mill became the focus of the Shriver brother-owned industrial complex. Together with a sawmill, cooper shop, blacksmith shop, and tannery the enterprises became known as "Union Mills."

Today, Union Mills grain products are stone-ground in the original brick grist mill of Andrew and David Shriver built in 1797. Fee. (301) 848-2288.

Montbray Wine Cellars, Limited. 818 Silver Run Valley Road, Silver Run. Continue north on Littlestown Pike (M-97) for a short distance to its intersection with Silver Run Valley Road. This impressive winery is nestled in the hills of Carroll County. Vineyards and wine cellars are open for tours year-round. Wine tastings are offered in conjunction with the tours. The proprietors recommend calling ahead for weekend information. Free. Fee for groups of 10 or more. (301) 346-7878.

GETTYSBURG, PA.

One of the greatest battles ever fought on this continent and one of the most decisive battles of world history took place here, in Gettysburg.

The Battle of Gettysburg began on July 1, 1863. Here, Gen. Robert E. Lee's Confederate Army of 75,000 men met the 97,000-man Union Army of Gen. George G. Meade. Confederates attacked the Northern troops through July 2, driving their opponents through Gettysburg to the heights south of town. However, the strength of this new position, coupled with Lee's poorly coordinated strategies, caused the Confederates to fail. There were enormous losses on both sides. On July 3, Lee made the fateful decision to attack the center of Meade's position on Cemetery Ridge. The Union defenders saw 15,000 Confederate soldiers lined shoulder to shoulder a mile and a half from end to end. In 50 minutes, 10,000 of the 15,000 men in the assault became casualties. With the failure of the attack, known as Pickett's Charge, the battle was over—the Union was preserved. There were 51,000 casualties . . . making Gettysburg the bloodiest battle of American History.

From Union Mills, continue northwest on M-97 across the Maryland-

Pennsylvania border. Continue now on P-97 (designated the Baltimore Pike) directly into Gettysburg.

WHERE TO GO

Visitor Center. Continue along the Baltimore Pike and enter the Gettysburg National Military Park. (The Baltimore Pike becomes Baltimore Street as it exits the park and enters Gettysburg proper.) To reach the Visitor Center, turn left off of the Baltimore Pike onto Hunt Avenue at Meade's Headquarters. Then turn right and drive north on Taneytown Road to the ample, free parking adjacent to the Visitor Center. You can also enter this area from Steinwehr Avenue. Begin your visit here for orientation and information and current events schedules. You will also find a large collection of Civil War artifacts and licensed guides here. The Electric Map orientation program is a 30-minute re-creation of the Battle of Gettysburg on a large relief map with colored lights and narration. Admission is free to the Visitor Center. A fee is charged for the Electric Map. Open daily. (717) 334-1124.

Cyclorama Center. Adjacent to the Visitor Center is the large (356 by 26 feet) painting of Pickett's Charge. Completed by artist Paul Philippoteaux in 1884, the painting is displayed with a dramatic sound and light show. The Cyclorama Center also has tour information and exhibits. A fee is charged to view the painting. Open daily. (717) 334-1124.

Self-Guided Auto Tour. This suggested 15-mile route begins at the Cyclorama Center and ends at the National Cemetery. Allow two hours to complete the tour. A free map and guidebook are available at the Visitor Center and the Cyclorama Center. Roads are open from 6 A.M. to 10 P.M., daily. (717) 334-1124.

Licensed Battlefield Guides. Originating from the Cyclorama Center, tour guides licensed by the National Park Service offer an opportunity for personal and in-depth tours of the battlefield. The two-hour tour accompanied by a guide is a good way to fully appreciate the events of Gettysburg. Fee. (717) 334-1124.

National Civil War Wax Museum. Steinwehr Avenue, Gettysburg. Well, if you didn't catch the whole story in the "larger than life" presentations at the Battlefield Park, stop here for all you ever wanted to know about Pickett's Charge. An animated figure of President Lincoln presents the Gettysburg Address. Fee. Call for hours. (717) 334-6245.

A. Lincoln's Place. 777 Baltimore Street, Gettysburg. Actor James A. Getty portrays Abraham Lincoln, live, at this theater. Check for a current performance schedule information. Fee. (717) 334-6049.

Soldiers National Museum is located on Baltimore Street, adjacent to A. Lincoln's Place. On display here are dioramas of the Civil War; life-size, animated human interest "Vignettes of History"; and an extensive collection of Civil War relics. Some visitors may remember that this collection was formerly Charley Weaver's Museum, named for the lovable character played by Cliff Arquette, a dedicated Civil War historian and actor. Open daily. Fee. (717) 334-4890.

NORTHWEST

Old Gettysburg Village of Quaint Shops. Located on Baltimore Street across from the Gettysburg Tour Center, is an opportunity to escape from the memories of the ravages of the Civil War into a fin, nostalgic visit to the past. A gift shop, country store, Amish shop, and ice cream store afford a shopping spree of treats and treasures.

The list of attractions in this area goes on and on with much of the focus on the Civil War. It is a fascinating destination on this day trip and one that may entice you to stay for an overnight visit. The Gettysburg Travel Council welcomes requests for information on the many attractions. Write 35 Carlisle Street, Gettysburg, PA., 17325, or call (717) 334-6274.

From Gettysburg, return to Baltimore by reversing the route of this day trip. Or, if time permits, you may want to pick up the York Pike (US-30) off of York Street in Gettysburg. From here, drive east into Lancaster, Pennsylvania, to sample the special Pennsylvania Dutch Country described in Day Trip 4 of the North section in this book. I-83 south becomes the most expedient route to Baltimore from here.

WHERE TO EAT

The Lampost Restaurant. 301 Carlisle Street, Gettysburg. Guests enjoy four dining rooms decorated in Early American fashion. This restaurant serves breakfast, lunch, and dinner and features sizzling steaks, country ham dinners, and a variety of seafood, all accompanied by homemade rolls, muffins, cakes, pies, and soups. Children's menu and small appetite menu available. Closed Christmas Day and New Year's Day. Reservations are advised. $-$$; no ☐. (717) 334-3313.

Jennie Wade Village Kitchen. 619 Baltimore Street. As you look out over the Old Gettysburg Village, enjoy delicious home-style cooking. The restaurant serves breakfast, lunch, and dinner, and snacks anytime, in a relaxing atmosphere. $-$$; no ☐. (717) 334-5648.

The Dobbin House Restaurant. 89 Steinwehr Avenue, Gettysburg. Early American cuisine is served here in this authentic colonial tavern (1776). Children's menu available. $$-$$$; ☐. Reservations are advised. (717) 334-2100.

WHERE TO STAY

Quality Inn, Gettysburg Motor Lodge. 380 Steinwehr Avenue. Located in town, it is 1 mile south of Center Square in Gettysburg. Ninety rooms, a heated pool, a cocktail lounge, and a putting green are among the amenities offered by the Inn and Lodge. It is within walking distance of restaurants, tours, and museums in the historic area. ☐. (717) 334-1103.

FESTIVALS AND CELEBRATIONS

JANUARY
Virginia
Alexandria. Children's Day. Play games with a tavern theme, learn bed-roping, and sample 18th-century fare at Gadsby's Tavern Museum. (703) 838-4242.

Alexandria. Lee Birthday Celebration. Joint celebration of the birthdays of "Light Horse Harry" Lee and his son, Robert E. Lee. (703) 548-8454.

FEBRUARY
Pennsylvania
Brandywine Valley. Maple Syrup Festival. Celebrated in the Tyler Arboretum in Lima. Maple trees are tapped for syrup and candy. Taste real syrup and hear Indian legends. (215) 566-9133.
Virginia
Alexandria. George Washington Birthday Parade. See the nation's largest parade celebrating the birthday of George Washington. (703) 549-0205.

Alexandria. Revolutionary War Encampment and Skirmish. Reenactments of Revolutionary and British 18th-century military camps with staged battle skirmishes. (703) 838-4848.

MARCH
Maryland
Thurmont. Maple Syrup Demonstrations. Tree-tapping, sap-boiling, and maple products for sale. Interpretations are given by the park ranger along with instructive films. (301) 271-7574.
Virginia
Mount Vernon. Annual Needlework Exhibit. More than 2,000 interna-

FESTIVALS AND CELEBRATIONS

tional needlework entries are displayed at the Woodlawn Plantation. Demonstrations. (703) 557-7880.

APRIL

Maryland
Accokeek. National Colonial Farm Day. Demonstrations and exhibits of 18th-century colonial agriculture and domestic life. (301) 283-2113.

Maryland. Maryland House and Garden Pilgrimage. Important houses and gardens throughout the state are opened to visitors. (301) 821-6933.

Sharpsburg. Easter Sunrise Service. Sunrise service at approximately 5:30 A.M. at Antietam Battlefield. Sponsored by the combined churches of Sharpsburg. (301) 432-5124.

Westminster. Opening Day—Kite Flying. Celebration of the opening day of the Carroll County Farm Museum with crafts, demonstrations of farm life, tours of the buildings, and nature trails. (301) 848-7775.

Pennsylvania
Chadds Ford. Pennsylvania Crafts Fair Day. Features traditional Pennsylvania craftsmen who demonstrate and sell their work in the Brandywine River Museum courtyard. (215) 459-1900.

Kennett Square. Easter Conservatory Displays. See an impressive array of Easter lilies and a variety of seasonal flowers. Concerts are scheduled each Sunday evening of the month-long event. (215) 388-6741.

Virginia
Arlington. Easter Sunrise Service, Arlington National Cemetery. The service is conducted by chaplains of several denominations with music provided by the Army Chorus and the Marine Corps Band. (703) 521-0072.

Leesburg. Oatlands Point-to-Point. Thoroughbred races at Oatlands Manor House and tours of the mansion are scheduled. (703) 777-2355.

MAY

Maryland
Aberdeen. Armed Forces Day Revolutionary battles re-created, modern weaponry demonstrated, skydiving, and military memorabilia at Ordnance Museum. (301) 278-3992.

Accokeek. Spring Farm Festival. Farm tours, wagon rides, plant sale, food and craft demonstrations. (301) 292-5665.

Bowie. Bowie Heritage Day. Free tours of Belair Mansion and Stables Museum, performances by Revolutionary War-era soldiers, slide presentations, and music. (301) 262-6200, extension 302.

Laurel. Montpelier Spring Festival. Arts and crafts, children's exhibits, band concerts, and food. (301) 776-2805.

FESTIVALS AND CELEBRATIONS

Westminster. Flower and Plant Market. All kinds of vegetable and flower plants, hanging baskets, herbs, shrubs, antiques, and tours of Union Mills Homestead and Grist Mill. (301) 848-2288 or (301) 848-6536.

Pennsylvania

Chadds Ford. Colonial Military Re-enactment. Re-creation of an 18th-century military camp with demonstrations of typical drills and colonial crafts, all staged at the Brandywine Battlefield State Park. (215) 459-3342.

Gettysburg. Memorial Day Parade and Service. Holiday parade and commemorative services are scheduled. (717)334-6274.

Gettysburg. Adams County Apple Blossom Festival. Orchard tours, crafts show, agricultural exhibits, apple butter boil, and plenty of home cookin' make this a "must do" for May. South Mountain Fair Grounds (10 miles north of Gettysburg). (717) 334-6274.

Virginia

Arlington. Memorial Day Service, Arlington National Cemetery. Presidential wreath-laying at the Tomb of the Unknown Soldier. (717) 521-0772.

JUNE

Maryland

Havre de Grace. Steppingstone Museum Crafts Fair. Demonstrations of authentic crafts of rural Harford County in the 1870–1910 period. (301) 939-2299.

Westminster. Carroll County Arts Day. Musical entertainment, crafts, art, country food, and tours of 19th-century farm house. (301) 848-7775.

Westminster. Flea Market and Square Dance. Antiques, crafts, square dance demonstrations and participation, and country food. (301) 848-7775.

Pennsylvania

Gettysburg. Civil War Heritage Days. Beginning in late June and extending into July is a nine-day Living History Encampment featuring authentic Civil War costumes, weaponry, and lifestyle. Contact: Gettysburg Travel Council, 35 Carlisle Street, Gettysburg, PA, 17325. (717) 334-6274.

Kennett Square. Illuminated Fountain Displays at Longwood Gardens are planned from June through August and include garden concerts. Contact: Longwood Gardens, US-1, Kennett Square, PA, 19348. (215) 388-6741.

Virginia

Alexandria. Alexandria Red Cross Waterfront Festival. Tall ships, marine exhibits, 10K race, fireworks, food, and boat races. Contact: Jane Brooks Mays, 401 Duke Street, Alexandria, VA, 22314. (703) 549-8300.

Lorton. Gunston Hall Arts and Crafts Celebration. 18th- and 19th-century arts and crafts demonstrated and sold, plus music and more. (703) 550-9220.

FESTIVALS AND CELEBRATIONS

West Virginia
Shepherdstown. The Great Rumsey Raft Race. Homemade-open-unlimited, rubber raft, canoe, and kayak races on the Potomac River. Contact: Eastern Gateway Travel Council, P.O. Box A, Harpers Ferry, WV, 25425. (304) 535-2482.

JULY

Maryland
Boonsboro. July 4th Fireworks. Annual fireworks at Washington Monument State Park. (301) 432-8065.

Westminster. Family Picnic Day. Music, clowns, games, crafts, antique car parade, horse and wagon rides, farm house tours, and fireworks are scheduled at the Carroll County Farm Museum. (301) 848-7775.

Westminster. Ice Cream Sundae Sunday. Outdoor summer festival featuring sundaes with homemade sauces, baked goods, helium balloons, and tours of the 1807 Shellman House. (301) 848-6494.

Pennsylvania
Kutztown. Kutztown Folk Festival. This event is a Pennsylvania Dutch extravaganza featuring indigenous cooking, crafts, music, and entertainment. The tiny town opens its heart and doors annually to the thousands of visitors who celebrate this event. (215) 683-8707.

Strasburg. Strasburg's Old-Time Independence Day Celebration. Pageant concluding with a fireworks display is planned. (717) 687-7691.

Virginia
Alexandria. Annual Virginia Scottish Games. Highland dancing, bagpipe bands, animal demonstrations, sports, and good food. (703) 549-0205.

AUGUST

Maryland
Havre de Grace. Art Show. Artists and craftsmen from the East Coast display their work; concessions. (301) 939-2296 or (301) 272-7500.

Havre de Grace. Seafood Festival. All you can eat: crabs, clams, fish, oysters, salads, watermelon, and more. (301) 939-4441 or (301) 273-6300.

Westminster. Flea Market and Chicken Fry. Country foods, nature trails, and more than 50 flea marketeers at Carroll County Farm Museum. (301) 848-7775.

Virginia
Alexandria. Annual Tavern Days. 18th-century tavern life re-created with food, drink, demonstrations, music, and children's activities. Contact: Gadsby's Tavern Museum, 134 N. Royal St., Alexandria, VA, 22314. (703) 838-4242.

FESTIVALS AND CELEBRATIONS

Leesburg. August Court Days. Re-enactment of 18th-century court term with crafts, musicians, and dancers. Contact: Evelyn Reynolds, 14 S. King St., Leesburg VA, 22075. (703) 777-2000.

Middleburg. Annual Virginia Wine Festival. Wine-tasting, grape-stomping, vineyard tours, and seminars. Contact: Vinifera Wine Growers Association, Box P, The Plains, VA, 22171. (703) 754-8564.

Manassas. Civil War Re-enactment. Living history camps, skirmish, and major battle, Civil War fashion show, crafts, and bluegrass music. Contact: Judy Jett, P.O. Box 495, Manassas, VA, 22110. (703) 368-4813.

SEPTEMBER

Maryland

Boonsboro. Boonesborough Days. More than 100 craftsmen featuring crafts show and sale, antiques, country store, entertainment, and food. (301) 582-2034.

Columbia. Maryland Renaissance Festival. Recreation of 16th-century fair with crafts, food, and pageantry entertainment. (301) 685-1445 or (301) 596-4673.

Havre de Grace. Fall Harvest Festival. Apple butter cooking, cider pressing, butter and cheese making, exhibits of food preservation, and entertainment at Steppingstone Museum. (301) 939-2299.

New Market. New Market Days. Country food, buggy rides, historical displays, and entertainment. (301) 831-6010.

Westminster. Smallwood Day Festival. Antique show and flea market with 200 dealers, crafts, continuous entertainment, and food. (301) 876-2553.

Pennsylvania

Chadds Ford. Brandywine Battlefield Re-enactment. 18th-century military encampments and mock-battle demonstrations at the Brandywine Battlefield State Park. (215) 459-3342.

Chadds Ford. Chadds Ford Days. Eighteenth-century country fair, costumed colonial craftsmen, live music, hayrides, meadow games, and great food are on the days' agenda. Don't miss "pigge and pippins"—pork and apples! (215) 388-7376.

West Virginia

Harpers Ferry. Mountain Heritage Arts and Crafts Festival. Crafts, Appalachian folk music, and festivities. (304) 725-2055.

OCTOBER

Maryland

Annapolis. Chesapeake Appreciation Days. Skipjack races, land exhibits,

FESTIVALS AND CELEBRATIONS

air show with antique aircraft, and great Maryland seafood make this a super annual event. (301) 757-4100.

Mount Airy. Berrywine Plantations October Wine Festival. Arts and crafts, with wine demonstrations, Italian food, and helicopter rides. (301) 662-8687.

St. Michaels. St. Michaels Seafood Festival. Local seafood, live entertainment, crab races, and fun contests. (301) 745-5056.

Thurmont. Catoctin Colorfest. Outdoor event featuring crafts, food, and fall foliage. (301) 271-4432.

Westminster. Fall Harvest Days. Nineteenth-century farming, quilting, broom-making, tinsmithing, and apple butter making at Carroll County Farm Museum. (301) 848-7775.

Virginia

Mt. Vernon. Annual Fall Festival of Needlework. Seminars, sherry, original kits, and tours. Contact: Woodlawn Plantation, P.O. Box 37, Mt. Vernon, VA, 22121. (703) 557-7880.

Waterford. Annual Waterford Homes Tour and Crafts Exhibit. National Historic Landmark village celebrates 18th-century style with music, demonstrations, and tours. Contact: Waterford Foundation, P.O. Box 142, Waterford, VA, 22190. (703) 882-3018.

NOVEMBER

Maryland

Easton. Waterfowl Festival. Decorative and working decoys, waterfowl art, Duck and Goose calling contest, antique guns, and auction. (301) 822-4567.

Westminster. Christmas Shop. Handcrafted gifts and tree trims from world markets and works of local crafts people are displayed at the Carroll County Farm Museum. (301) 848-7775.

Pennsylvania

Chadds Ford. A wide variety of traditional experiences and seasonal events celebrate the Christmas holidays. Beginning in November and extending to January, model train gardens, decorated trees, and best-loved winter scenes painted by the Wyeth family are displayed at the Brandywine River Museum. (215) 459-1900.

Kennett Square. Chrysanthemum Festival. Fifteen thousand spectacular mums are displayed indoors, and a festival of musical performances and craft demonstrations is in the American harvest tradition at Longwood Gardens. (215) 388-6741.

Virginia

Leesburg. Christmas at Oatlands. Authentic 1880s decorations adorn the plantation manor house. (703) 777-3174.

Delaware

Winterthur Museum and Gardens. "Yuletide at Winterthur." Begin-

FESTIVALS AND CELEBRATIONS

ning in November and extending to the end of December, see 21 of the museum's rooms re-create traditions of early holiday entertainment. (302) 654-1548.

DECEMBER
Maryland

Annapolis. Christmas in Annapolis. Open house tours, museum houses with special events, concerts, feasting, pub crawls, and caroling. Contact: Tourism Council of Annapolis and Anne Arundel County, 171 Conduit St., Annapolis, MD, 21401. (301) 268-TOUR.

Ellicott City. Old Fashioned Christmas Gardens. Trains and displays back to 1930s, HO-gauge model railroad depicting the first 13 miles of the B&O. (301) 461-1944.

Hagerstown. Miller House Christmas. Federal period townhouses decked in holiday decor of fresh greens, large Christmas trees. (301) 797-8782.

Havre de Grace. Havre de Grace Candlelight Tour. Tour of historic town, including museums, homes, and businesses. (301) 939-3947.

Kensington. Kensington Christmas Open House. Christmas decorations, strolling carolers, and open house in antique dealers' community. (301) 946-8666.

Westminster. Christmas Open House and Candle Lighting Ceremony. Candlelight tours, decorations, old-fashioned Christmas trees, and carolers at Carroll County Farm Museum. (301) 848-7775.

Pennsylvania

Kennett Square. Longwood Gardens Christmas Display. Get your Christmas spirit here! See more than 2,000 poinsettias in the heated conservatory and a magnificent Christmas tree exhibition. Outside, 35,000 lights adorn 80 trees. Music and choral concerts each evening. (215) 388-6741.

Strasburg. Twelve Days of Christmas. Madrigal music accompanies a traditional feast designed around the well-known song. Each course relates to the gifts in the verses. The King and Queen are present to welcome you, along with court jesters and a suckling pig. Located at the Historic Strasburg Inn. Reservations are recommended. (717) 687-7691.

Ephrata. Ephrata Cloister. Live, theatrical improvisations of cloister life with period costumes. Special candlelight Christmas tour. (717) 733-4811.

Lancaster. Victorial Christmas at Wheatland. Candlelight tour of James Buchanan's historic 1828 mansion residence, decorated for the

FESTIVALS AND CELEBRATIONS

holidays in Victorian style. Tours by guides in period costumes. (717) 392-8721.

Virginia

Alexandria. Scottish Christmas Walk. Parade with bagpipers and clans, concerts, house tours, antiques, and crafts displays are among the fantastic festivities. (703) 549-0205.

Alexandria. Scottish New Year's Eve. Hogmanay with Scottish food and entertainment, midnight ceremony. Advance reservations are required. (703) 549-0205.

Alexandria. Old Town Christmas Candlelight Tour. Five historic properties are decorated for the holidays and open for tours. Refreshments and period music are planned. (703) 549-0205.

Lorton. Carols by Candlelight at Gunston Hall Plantation. 18th-century music, caroling, and refreshments. (703) 550-9220.

Mount Vernon. Carols by Candlelight at Woodlawn Plantation. Nineteenth-century Yuletide musicians and madrigalists with period music. (703) 557-7880.

West Virginia

Harpers Ferry. Old Tyme Christmas. Authentic celebration of the mid-1800s with natural decorations and music make this a worthwhile holiday event. (304) 535-2354.

THE GREAT OUTDOORS

STATE PARKS AND ADDITIONAL INFORMATION
WEST VIRGINIA: For Park and forest information, reservations, hunting and fishing information, and other data relating to outdoor recreation, call (304) 348-2764 or write:

West Virginia Department of Natural Resources
Division of Parks and Recreation
State Capitol—SP
Charleston, WV 25305

WASHINGTON, D.C., AREA-MARYLAND-NATIONAL CAPITAL PARK AND PLANNING COMMISSION: For information, write:

Parkside Headquarters
9500 Brunett Avenue
Silver Spring, MD 20901
For park permits and information call (301) 565-7417.

VIRGINIA: Information is available at all Virginia Highway Information centers. Information and reservations are available from:

Virginia Division of Parks and Recreation-Central Office
1201 Washington Building
Capitol Square
Richmond, VA 23219
For information, call (804) 786-2132. Camping reservations are available from *Ticketron Reservation Center*, (804) 490-3939.

THE GREAT OUTDOORS

MARYLAND: Maps, winter activities, camping, hunting, and fishing information are available from:

Maryland Forest and Park Service
Department of Natural Resources
Tawes State Office Building
Annapolis, MD 21401
Phone (301) 269-3771, TTY for deaf (Baltimore) 269-2609, TTY (statewide) 1-800-492-5062.

PENNSYLVANIA: General state park information, maps, and pamphlets relating to specific parks are available from:

Office of Public Information
Department of Environmental Resources
Harrisburg, PA 17120
Phone (717) 787-2657

DELAWARE: Tourism and campground information is available from:

Delaware State Travel Service
99 Kings Highway
P.O. Box 1401
Dover, DE 19903
Phone 1-(800) 441-8846

Boating and fishing information can be obtained from:

Division of Fish and Wildlife
99 Kings Highway
P.O. Box 1401
Dover, DE 19903
Phone (302) 736-3440

SEASONAL INFORMATION

Baltimore Office of Promotion and Tourism
110 West Baltimore Street
Baltimore, Maryland 21201   (301) 752-8632

Maryland Division of Tourist Development
1748 Forest Drive
Annapolis, Maryland 21401   (301) 269-2686

Department of Travel Development
Commonwealth of Pennsylvania
Department of Commerce
Forum Building
Harrisburg, Pennsylvania 17120
(717) 787-5453 or 1-800- A-FRIEND

Delaware State Travel Service
Delaware Development Office
99 Kings Highway, P.O. Box 1401
Dover, Delaware 19903   (302)736-4271

Virginia Division of Tourism
Commonwealth of Virginia
Bell Tower on Capitol Square
101 North Ninth Street
Richmond, Virginia 23219   (804) 786-4484

Governor's Office of Economic and Community Development
Travel Development Division
Charleston, West Virginia 25305
(304) 348-2286 or 1-800-624-9110

REGIONAL INFORMATION

NORTH

Day Trips 1 and 2
Baltimore County Tourism Committee
Baltimore County Chamber of Commerce
100 West Pennsylvania Avenue
Towson, Maryland 21204   (301)825-6200

Day Trip 3
Lebanon Valley Tourist and Visitors Bureau
1650 North Seventh Street
Lebanon, Pennsylvania 17042   (717) 272-8555

Day Trip 4
Pennsylvania Dutch Visitors Bureau
1799 Hempstead Road
Lancaster, Pennsylvania 17601   (717) 299-8901.

Day Trip 5
Berks County Pennsylvania Dutch Travel Association
Sheraton Berkshire Inn
Route 422 West, Paper Mill Road Exit
Wyomissing, Pennsylvania 19610   (215) 375-4085

REGIONAL INFORMATION

NORTHEAST

Day Trip 1
Discover Harford County
P.O. Box 635
Bel Air, Maryland 21014   (301) 939-1122

Cecil County Office of Planning and Economic Development
Room 300, Court House
Elkton, Maryland 21921   (301) 398-0200, Ext. 144

Day Trip 2
Delaware Development Office
Delaware State Travel Service
99 Kings Highway, P.O. Box 1401
Dover, Delaware 19903   (302) 736-4271.

Day Trip 3
Philadelphia Convention and Visitors Bureau
Three Penn Center Plaza
Philadelphia, Pennsylvania 19102   (215) 568-6599

Day Trip 4
Chester County Tourist Promotion Bureau
33 West Market Street
West Chester, Pennsylvania 19380   (215) 431-6365

SOUTHEAST

Day Trip 1
Tourism Council of Annapolis and Anne Arundel County
171 Conduit Street
Annapolis, Maryland 21401   (301) 263-5357 or (301) 268-TOUR

Day Trips 2 and 3
Tourism Council of the Upper Chesapeake
P.O. Box 66
Centreville, Maryland 21617   (301) 758-2300

REGIONAL INFORMATION

SOUTH

Day Trip 1
Tri-County Council for Southern Maryland
P.O. Box 1634
Charlotte Hall, Maryland 20622 (301) 884-2144

Day Trip 2
Prince George's Travel Promotion Council, Inc.
6600 Kenilworth Avenue
Riverdale, Maryland 20840 (301) 927-0700

SOUTHWEST and Washington Region

Day Trip 1
Montgomery County Office of Economic Development
Executive Office Building
101 Monroe Street, Suite 1500
Rockville, Maryland 20850 (301) 251-2345

Howard County Tourism Council
Overlook Center, Suite 401
5457 Twin Knolls Road
Columbia, Maryland 21045 (301) 730-7817

Day Trips 2 and 3
Prince George's Travel Promotion Council Inc.
6600 Kenilworth Avenue
Riverdale, Maryland 20840 (301) 927-0700

Day Trip 4
Washington, D.C. Convention and Visitors Association
1575 Eye Street, N.W.
Washington, D.C. 20005 (202) 789-7000

Day Trip 5
Fairfax County Chamber of Commerce
10856 Main Street
Fairfax, Virginia 22030 (703) 591-5550

REGIONAL INFORMATION

Alexandria Tourist Council
221 King Street
Alexandria, Virginia 22314   (703) 549-0205

Greater Manassas Chamber of Commerce
9100 Center Street
P.O. Box 495
Manassas, Virginia 22110   (703) 368-4813

Day Trip 6

Montgomery County Office of Economic Development
Executive Office Building
101 Monroe Street, Suite 1500
Rockville, Maryland 20850   (301) 251-2345

Day Trip 7

Loudon County Visitor Center
16 West Loudon Street
Leesburg, Virginia 22075   (703) 777-0519

WEST

Day Trip 1

Howard County Tourism Council
Overlook Center, Suite 401
5457 Twin Knolls Road
Columbia, Maryland 21045   (301) 730-7817

Tourism Council of Frederick County, Inc.
19 East Church Street
Frederick, Maryland 21701   (301) 663-8687

Day Trip 2

Tourism Council of Frederick County, Inc.
19 East Church Street
Frederick, Maryland 21701   (301) 663-8687

Day Trip 3

Washington County Tourism Division
Court House Annex
Hagerstown, Maryland 21740   (301) 791-3130

REGIONAL INFORMATION

Tourism Council of Frederick County, Inc.
19 East Church Street
Frederick, Maryland 21701   (301) 663-8687

Day Trip 4
Eastern Gateway Travel Council Inc.
P.O. Box A
Harpers Ferry, West Virginia 25425   (304) 535-2482

Tourism Council of Frederick County, Inc.
19 East Church Street
Frederick, Maryland 21701   (301) 663-8687

NORTHWEST

Day Trip 1
Carroll County Office of Information, Tourism and Promotion
County Office Building, Room 301
225 North Center Street
Westminster, Maryland 21157   (301) 876-2085

Day Trip 2
Tourism Council of Frederick County, Inc.
19 Church Street
Frederick, Maryland 21701   (301) 663-8687

Day Trip 3
Carroll County Office of Information, Tourism and Promotion
County Office Building, Room 301
225 Center Street
Westminster, Maryland 21157   (301) 876-2085

Adams County
Gettysburg Travel Council
35 Carlisle Street
Gettysburg, Pennsylvania 17325   (717) 334-6274

East Woods Press Books

American Bed & Breakfast
   Cook Book, The
Backcountry Cooking
Berkshire Trails for Walking & Ski Touring
Best Bed & Breakfast in the World, The
Blue Ridge Mountain Pleasures
California Bed & Breakfast
Campfire Chillers
Campfire Songs
Canoeing the Jersey Pine Barrens
Carolina Curiosities
Carolina Seashells
Carpentry: Some Tricks of the Trade from
   an Old-Style Carpenter
Catfish Cookbook, The
Charlotte: A Touch of Gold
Complete Guide to Backpacking
   in Canada
Creative Gift Wrapping
Day Trips From Baltimore
Day Trips From Cincinnati
Day Trips From Houston
Drafting: Tips and Tricks on Drawing and
   Designing House Plans
Exploring Nova Scotia
Fifty Years on the Fifty:
   The Orange Bowl Story
Fructose Cookbook, The
Grand Old Ladies
Grand Strand: An Uncommon Guide
   to Myrtle Beach, The
Healthy Trail Food Book, The
Hiking from Inn to Inn
Hiking Virginia's National Forests
Historic Country House Hotels
Hosteling USA, Third Edition
How to Afford Your Own Log Home
How to Play With Your Baby
Indiana: Off the Beaten Path
Interior Finish: More Tricks of the Trade
Just Folks: Visitin' with Carolina People
Kays Gary, Columnist
Maine Coast: A Nature Lover's
   Guide, The
Making Food Beautiful
Mid-Atlantic Guest House Book, The
New England Guest House Book, The
New England: Off the Beaten Path
Ohio: Off the Beaten Path
Parent Power!
Parks of the Pacific Coast
Race, Rock and Religion
River Reflections
Rocky Mountain National Park Hiking Trails
Saturday Notebook, The

Sea Islands of the South
Separation and Divorce in North Carolina
South Carolina Hiking Trails
Southern Guest House Book, The
Southern Rock: A Climber's Guide
   to the South
Sweets Without Guilt
Tar Heel Sights: Guide to North Carolina's
   Heritage
Tennessee Trails
Toys That Teach Your Child
Train Trips: Exploring America by Rail
Trout Fishing the Southern Appalachians
Vacationer's Guide to Orlando and
   Central Florida, A
Walks in the Catskills
Walks in the Great Smokies
Walks with Nature in Rocky Mountain
   National Park
Whitewater Rafting in Eastern America
Wildflower Folklore
Woman's Journey, A
You Can't Live on Radishes

Order from:

The East Woods Press
429 East Boulevard
Charlotte, NC 28203